Leabharlanna Poiblí Chathair Bhaile Átha Cliath
Dublin City Public Libraries
Baile Munna

Comhairle Cathrach
Bhaile Átha Cliath
Dublin City Council
Ballymun

Tel: 8421890

Due Date	Due Date	Due Date

Advice for the Dying*

Also by Sallie Tisdale

Advice for the Dying*

A Practical Perspective on Death

*And Those Who Love Them

Sallie Tisdale

ALLEN&UNWIN

First published in Great Britain in 2018 by Allen & Unwin
First published in the United States in 2018 by Touchstone, an imprint of Simon &
Schuster, Inc., under the title *Advice for Future Corpses*

Allen & Unwin
c/o Atlantic Books
Ormond House
26–27 Boswell Street
London WC1N 3JZ

Phone: 020 7269 1610
Fax: 020 7430 0916
Email: UK@allenandunwin.com
Web: www.allenandunwin.com/uk

A CIP catalogue record for this book is available from the British Library.

Internal design by Jill Putorti

Hardback ISBN 978 1 76063 270 0
E-Book ISBN 978 1 76063 989 1

Printed in Great Britain by TJ International ltd, Padstow, Cornwall

10 9 8 7 6 5 4 3 2 1

For Carol, who taught me to be weightless;
Kyogen, who reminded me that it might come as a surprise;
Stephanie, who never quit;
Marc, who kept laughing;
Butch, who found his way to the sunshine;
and Mom, who was a good woman.

That was the best ice cream soda I ever tasted.

—LAST WORDS OF LOU COSTELLO

Contents

1

Dangerous Situation

Right now: imagine dying. Make it what you want. You could be in your bedroom, on a lonesome hill, or in a beautiful hotel. Whatever you want. What is the season? What time of day is it? Perhaps you want to lie in sweet summer grass and watch the sun rise over the ocean. Imagine that. Perhaps you want to be cuddled in a soft bed, listening to Mozart—or Beyoncé. Do you want to be alone? Is there a particular hand you want to hold? Do you smell the faint scent of baking bread—or Chanel No. 19? Close your eyes. Feel the grass. The silk sheets. The skin of the loving hand. Hear the long-held note. Dance a little. Smell the bread. Imagine that.

I have never died, so this entire book is a fool's advice. Birth and death are the only human acts we cannot practice. We love our murder mysteries, and how we love our video games, but death looms ahead as a kind of theory. In Victorian times, children were kept away from anything regarding sex or birth, but they sat at deathbeds, witnessed deaths, and helped with the care of the body. Now children may watch the birth of a sibling and never see a dead body. But neither do most adults; many people reach the end of their own lives having never seen a dying person.

One day when I was seven, my mother sat at the dining table and cried all afternoon, even though it was almost Christmas. My father told me that my grandfather had died. I wasn't sure what that meant. I liked Grandpa, who laughed a lot and took his dentures out at the dinner table to make the kids scream. My mother started packing a suitcase. She was going to the funeral, he said. I didn't know that word, but if my mother was going out of town alone, it had to be something special. "Can I go, too?" I asked. "No," he said, sharply. I was not allowed. Funerals were not for children. No one explained, and I never saw Grandpa again.

As an adult, I've tried to see death as clearly as I can. This was less a deliberate choice than the natural path my life took. Perhaps the long-ago echoing mystery of my grandfather's disappearance had something to do with it. Several paths have woven around each other to form my life, and, seen as a braid—as a whole life, and not pieces—I see the similarities, the shared focus. As a writer, I have to be willing to investigate myself and the world without flinching. As a nurse and an end-of-life educator, I must be willing to step inside the personal world of others, to step inside secrets, hold another's pain. I'm a Buddhist practitioner and teacher, and lead workshops about preparing for death from a Buddhist perspective. This practice requires a ruthless self-examination and a deep study of how I create my world. Together, these strands have given me a measure of equanimity about the inevitable sea of change that is a human life. They have fed each other and taught me to tolerate ambiguity, discomfort of many kinds, and intimacy—which is sometimes the most uncomfortable thing of all. In thinking about death in all its ramifications, these lessons are a great help, and death is a help in deepening all these lessons. I know what to do at the bedside of a dying person, and I know a lot of practical information about what works when we are preparing to die or to lose someone we love. The most important experience I've had is one most of us share: the deaths of people I love. I know grief.

I can depend on these varied skills to meet a new situation the way an electrician can read wiring in a house he's entering for the first time. But even though death is not unfamiliar to me, I don't want to sound as though dying and death are ordinary. What all these things have taught me is that dying and death will always be extraordinary.

When he was dying, the contemporary Buddhist teacher Dainin Katagiri wrote a remarkable and dense book called *Returning to Silence*. Life, he wrote, "is a dangerous situation." It is the frailty of life that makes it precious; his words are suffused with the blunt fact of his own life passing away. "The china bowl is beautiful because sooner or later it will break.... The life of the bowl is always existing in a dangerous situation." Such is our struggle: this precarious beauty. This inevitable wound. We forget—how easily we forget—that love and loss are intimate companions, that we love the real flower so much more than the plastic one, love the evanescence of autumn's brilliant colors, the cast of twilight across a mountainside lasting only a moment. It is this very fragility that opens our hearts.

Funerals are not for children. We learn by details, by the tiniest word or grimace. I grew up in a ranching and logging community, and my father was a firefighter. People died in the mills; people died in fires. People died on the rivers and in the mountains and on their ranches. Accidents happened. When I was growing up, we had a primitive cabin in the forest where my family would spend weeks each summer. I learned to fish for my breakfast and eat trout whole, the head and tail in my hands, and examined the little dead animals I would find here and there. From a young age I was drawn to an inquiry of bodies, of living things, which inevitably meant a study of predation and decay. I kept all kinds of pets: lizards and snakes I caught in the hills, chameleons and praying mantises I sent for in the mail, and once a baby alligator I was given. I had to feed my pets, and most preferred live food, so I fed them crickets, mealworms, grasshoppers. I liked grasshoppers and even kept them as pets sometimes, but I happily fed them to my mantises. The chameleons always died; the mantises always died. Their seasons are short. The alligator died quickly; I had no idea what it really needed. I tried to embalm it, with limited success—just good enough for a memorable presentation at show-and-tell. When one of my turtles died, my brother and I buried it in my mother's rose bed to see if we could get an empty turtle shell, because we knew this would be quite a good thing to have. But when we dug it up a few weeks later, there was almost nothing left. The shell that had seemed so solid and permanent turned out to be another kind of flesh, and its decay left me with a strange, disturbed feeling. The earth had proved to be fiercer than I had guessed. Grandpa died. Our dog died. I saw my first dead body at the age of fourteen when I attended the funeral of a classmate, the first of several peers to die over the next few years. Funerals are not for children, I was told, but that didn't have anything to do with my exposure to death.

In my sophomore year in college, I took Anatomy and Physiology. It was a yearlong course intended to fulfill the requirements for premed. In the lab, we worked with four cadavers that had been dissected in different ways by senior students. The faces were always covered. Dr. Welton, a tall, bald, solemn man with a photographic memory, tolerated no jokes. Our hours in the laboratory were quiet and serious. We carried our worksheets from one table to the other, tracing lines, lifting tags, examining the exquisite textures, the lovely complications of bodies. I was seventeen, fascinated by biology, and I found anatomy to be a great wonder. Each of these bodies was more or less the same in every detail, so similar that detailed maps to the tiniest structures could be made. Yet each of these bodies was unique as well. And all this complex machinery worked. Or had worked, which was part of the lesson.

I made myself a nuisance in the A & P lab, and then in Dr. Welton's office, showering him with questions until he gave me extra work just to shut me up. In the second term, I was allowed to do dissection. This meant letting myself into the locked cadaver laboratory after classes. The room was always cool and quiet, scented with formaldehyde and the faint leathery smell of the bodies. The lower windows were covered in paper to keep out prying eyes, and the room was lit with the dissipated sunshine of late afternoon. Dr. Welton assigned me to the newest body, where dissection had just begun, and specifically to the left hand. He wanted tendons and ligaments exposed. Day after day, I took my tools and sat alone beside the table and carefully opened the hand, following diagrams in a thick book. I did a good job. I gradually came to understand that hand, and all hands, in a way that remains with me now. But I came to understand something else as well. One day, I had almost finished exposing the tendons. I found that by pulling on them gently, I could move the fingers one by one. I had never been uneasy in that room, but that day I looked up the length of the body, naked except for the covered face, and all at once I was covered in goose bumps.

Dissection is more a psychological experience than an intellectual one for many people. I found it to be both. I remember more about how it felt to be with the dead, to touch and open a body, to see what happens to bodies, than any details about the insertion of the latissimus dorsi muscle. (I learned that, too, in a way I could never have learned from books.) Working with cadavers makes it clear what death *is*. A subject becomes an object. A person becomes a body. And, miraculously, turns *back*: this body, this firm, immobile object, is, was, a person, a warm, breathing person. A body is not an ordinary object—can never be an ordinary object. This particular object had once been awake.

With a jolt, I realized that what I was cutting apart had been a living hand, just like mine; that it had been pliant and animated. It had held a pen, shoveled dirt, bathed a child, stroked someone's hair. That it was like my precious hands, which until that moment had simply been part of me. Alive. I realized, *This man is like me.* I already knew that this body was like my body; I could label its parts. But suddenly I knew that this *man* was like me. And that I would be like this man.

We share a grand social agreement about mortality. We choose not to notice, if we can. I was born in the United States in 1957, the largest cohort of baby boomers. We've been a most fortunate generation, and also one of the most delusional. We are energetically trying not to be as old as we are, to not look old, feel old, and, most of all, to not be perceived as old. The worship of an ideal, youthful immortality is nothing new: the Greeks were obsessed with it, and perhaps all humans are, to some extent. But my generation seems both more protected from the fact of aging and less resigned to it. We spin our mornings and evenings away, concentrating on the body, our body, my body, without actually looking very deeply at *body* and all it means. We pretend that what we absolutely know to be true somehow isn't true. But the nasty surprises can't really be avoided: the midget varicosities, the bald spots, the speckling, the softening—in Emerson's words, "Nature is so insulting in her hints & notices." I am sometimes confounded by this generation of my peers that seems to have surrendered to a marketplace of diets, remedies, visualizations, trademarked mindfulness for every trouble, medication for every mood, as though . . . what? What do we think will happen instead?

I feel lucky to have had early encounters with the dead, even though I sought them out for my own inchoate reasons. A few years after the cadaver lab, the bodies at rest became living bodies again when I started working as an aide in a large nursing home. Many of the people in my family have lived long lives, well into their nineties. Perhaps because I had grown up knowing one set of great-grandparents, all my grandparents, and many elderly aunts and uncles, I had not learned to be afraid of the old. Their slumping, softening bodies with white hair, matronly bosoms, and grizzled chins were familiar to me. They just were what they were: different from me, very different, but not bad. Not wrong and not hidden, just different.

I watch nurse's aides now and don't know how they do it; the labor is hard and long and pays a fraction of what you think an enlightened society would pay for such important work. I loved that job: I had a uniform, my first paycheck; I was in love and filled with boundless energy. Part of what I was learning was the culture of a profession, the vocabulary and belief system. At first I was learning the particular skills of caring for fragile people: the rituals of the infirm. There is a right way to make a bed around a person, to bathe a person who cannot help you, to move a person in and out of a wheelchair when she can't stand. I watched a person die for the first time in that job and helped to wash her body, and learned there is a right way to do that. I don't remember any moment of clarity in those years, of starkly knowing that this old man, that tiny, wrinkled woman, had once been like me. I didn't wonder whether I would one day be like them any more than I thought I might be like my Aunt Lois. I was smooth-skinned and full of stamina, and I liked the work, and didn't think much beyond that.

When I knew that I was going to be a writer, I knew I wanted a regular job to support myself, one that had nothing to do with writing. Nursing made sense. The hours were flexible, the pay was good, and I could work part-time. The surprise wasn't how much harder the training and job turned out to be than I expected: such is the amateur's lesson in any profession. The surprise that snuck up on me without warning was how taking care of people's bodies and minds in such a concrete way would inevitably seep into how I myself lived in the world. I was too young to know that the work I did would color the way I saw my own life and my own body at least as much as the cadavers did. I was too young to realize how young I was.

Thirty-odd years later, I work a few days a week in a pal-

liative care program with people who have serious chronic illnesses. I see hardy old people who are doing well and fragile
people younger than me. About a fifth of our clients die every
year. My clients live all over the city, in apartments and trailers,
in memory care units, in sprawling assisted-living complexes,
and in adult foster homes, part of the state's extensive network.
People like my clients are everywhere in the world; how could
they not be? I forget that this part of life is so hidden, because
when I go to work, that's where I am: in that memory care unit
where, really, anything could happen; in that small home where
five very old women are cared for by several younger women; in
that assisted-living building where every apartment is a micro-
cosm of a long life.

But for many years, I forgot that I was like the man whose hand
I had opened like a rose. We do forget such things when we are
young, if we are lucky enough to learn them at all. I forgot that I
would get old and lose the power that seemed entirely part of me,
the power that allowed me to be busy and productive, rear three
children, write books in the evening, and still get up and go to
work. When I thought about death in those years, I didn't quite
believe in it. Of course patients sometimes died. People I didn't
know died—people on the news, people in the hospital, people
on the street. My old relatives began to die, one after the other.
But they were, after all, really old.

When I was in my early twenties, just finishing nursing school, I
started practicing Soto Zen Buddhism. This is not a book about
a Buddhist approach to dying. But my life is deeply informed
by Buddhism, and I will return to its vocabulary and guidance

throughout. The first story Buddhists learn—the root story—is that of the historical Buddha, Siddhartha. He was a pampered prince who grew up carefully protected from any painful sights. When he grew restless and slipped away from his bodyguards, he saw several things he had never seen before: a sick person, an old person, and then a corpse. His retainer told him that this was inevitable, that such things happen to everyone. What a shock for the young prince. *Every*one? *Me?* Then he saw an ascetic, a religious practitioner who had withdrawn from the world in order to seek knowledge. The prince then knew his life's task was to understand the meaning of the inevitability of change. (In some versions of the story, these terrible sights are sent by the gods in order to goad him into seeking enlightenment.)

Buddhist practice requires one to confront the blunt facts of life: that we are constantly changing, that we are dissatisfied more or less all the time, that we try desperately to hang on to what we have. That we are mortal, suffering beings. We will change and everything and everyone we love will change. An old Buddhist meditation is simply this: *I am of the nature to grow old. I am of the nature to be sick. I am of the nature to die. All that is dear to me and everyone I love are of the nature to change. There is no way to escape being separated from them.* The historical Buddha's story has resonated so deeply with millions of us over thousands of years because it is our own. Sooner or later we each have such an epiphany: sickness, aging, death. Perhaps the sick person gets well and the old person is a stranger and the corpse is carefully made up and lying in an expensive casket in a church, but *still*. At some point you think, *Me? Me too?* And you either turn from that thought or start looking for an explanation. Either way, the epiphany has a way of returning.

One of the central ideas of our lives is that there will be a tomorrow. *Tomorrow* may be when I get the laundry done. *Tomorrow* may come after I retire. *Tomorrow* I start summer vacation. But if we are aware of our dangerous situation, there is no tomorrow. No next year. Only this. Of course we plan anyway; there's no other way to live than to plant seeds and wait for the fruit, whether it's the laundry or retirement or next summer's vacation. The trick comes in planning next summer's vacation while knowing that next summer is not promised to anyone. This impermanence is the key to our pain and our joy. What a radical acceptance of things as they are! "Why should we treat ourselves in a special way?" asked Shunryu Suzuki. "When you understand birth and death as the birth and death of everything—plants, animals and trees—it is not a problem anymore. A problem for everything is not a problem anymore." A table is a table because of its shape and how we use it, and because there is a chair, and because we call it a table. We can take a table apart, and at some point it is no longer a table. Even if all the parts are there, the table is gone, because no table exists apart from how it fits together. I am like this; you are like this. Everything is like this. Such knowledge can give us a vast space in which to live our lives, a freedom within life. A problem for everyone is no longer a problem. We will break, as all things will; how beautiful, how sweet. How hard.

People have been wondering about the nature of death for all the eons we have been able to wonder. The modern literature of death never allows us to forget Cicero, who is otherwise rarely mentioned in conversation: "To philosophize is to get ready to die." The impulse is to lean on history a little, add context, make a bigger picture. But do we really need to add weight to this conversation? I will do it, too, now and then—depend on another's words. Perhaps I'm just reminding myself that all of our questions have been asked before. In the workshops I lead, the same questions come up every time: pain, dignity, fear. Old, old questions. How do we prepare for something so mysterious, so unseen? How do we make decisions about the unknown? How can we prepare for the inevitable when we aren't sure we even believe in it?

We talk about death as a remote idea, imagine what we would like our dying to be like, and do this casually over a few beers, on a summer evening when the air is sweet and our healthy child hums quietly at our feet. We talk about dying when to die seems like a complete impossibility, and so can be considered.

Look around the room—right now. Wherever you are: the office, the subway, your living room. Look around, all around, at everything you can see. You are going to die in one minute. That's it. There's no time to find the sweet summer grass or your favorite Adele song. No hand to hold. No time to make a call or write a note. What you see right now, right here—this season, these people, this day, this light, and this room—that's what you have.

My friend Carol had rarely been sick in her life; she didn't even catch colds. She was a criminal lawyer in rural Oregon. When she ran for election as county judge, she spent weeks knocking on doors and introducing herself to voters. By the time she was elected—the first woman judge in Yamhill County—her left leg was numb. She assumed she had a pinched nerve, that she'd walked too much, had been wearing the wrong shoes.

Then she called me and said, "I have cancer." No preamble. Lots of tears. Our bodies are, by any measure, miraculously complex homeostatic systems. But they are also flimsy entropies, and much of what they do is silent: the whispering aneurysm, the invisible embolus, the dying cell, the multiplying cell. Her routine mammogram the summer before had been clean, but now Carol had metastatic breast cancer. The numb leg was caused by an abdominal tumor pressing on her spine.

People with terminal illnesses talk about the knowledge as a kind of border. Life is divided into the time before and the time after one knows one is dying—*really* knows. The day will come when we cross the border between theory and fact. People are often quite pragmatic in the first days. Paul Kalanithi was a neurosurgeon when he was diagnosed with lung cancer. He and his wife, Lucy, lay in his hospital bed together, talking it out. "I told her to remarry, that I couldn't bear the thought of her being alone. I told her we should refinance the mortgage immediately." This temporary acceptance, this willingness, is common; perhaps it is protective, a kind of endorphin buffer to the shock. Carol told me later that she thought she might never leave the hospital. She was calm there, in a private room facing west into her beloved coastal mountains, and the sun fell across her bed and she allowed herself to be what she so suddenly was: not a lawyer, not a judge or wife or dog lover, but a patient with a terminal illness. We talked a little about her biopsy, her options, and a bit more about her dogs and what might happen to them.

Like endorphins, this acceptance wears off. Carol had surgery, recovered, was sworn in as a judge, and took the bench with gusto. She responded well to chemotherapy and lived for several more years. She did anything and everything she could not to die, but she was dying the entire time. She knew it. I knew it. Every day was the day after.

This is a book about preparing for your own death and for the deaths of people close to you. I am talking about both these experiences, so sometimes I am addressing you the visitor, the loved one. And sometimes I am addressing you the dying one. (I am always addressing myself.) Most of us in the West will die in our old age of chronic illnesses, and most of those illnesses cause a decline toward death over months or years. A lot of what I am saying is addressed to this fact: that you and I are likely to die over a period of time from disease, and before that happens, we will see family and friends die this way. But I have seen people die quickly. I've seen people die in an instant. I believe that if we are able to consider death, our own death (me? really?)—if we can become familiar with the fact of death—then minutes are enough. We know from a thousand shining moments how time speeds up and slows down. If we are ready to look at it squarely, perhaps five seconds is enough. We spend our lives creating our future, by creating habits, learning from experience, examining our weaknesses and strengths. Our lives as we live them day by day create the person we will be at the moment of death. You see this at the bedside of a dying person. You see it in the way a body rests or fights, in the lines of the face, in the faint shadow of a smile or a scowl, worry or peace. With every passing day, we create the kind of death we will have.

In this book, I look at how we grieve, what can be done with the body that remains, and the strange, undeniable fact that the presence of death can be joyful. What exactly are we afraid of? What is a good death? What really happens in the weeks and months before death? What does it look like when a person dies, and after? There are brief sections of practical advice, a little Buddhism, a few stories of deaths and preparing for death. I want this book to make you think about a few things you don't really want to think about.

Dying people make symbolic statements. One of the most common images people use is traveling. A dying person may become excited, even frantic, and say he is looking for his passport, must find his luggage, must hurry to catch a train. Human minds share symbols and this one is so apt and easy to understand. How do you get ready to die? The same way you prepare for a trip to a place you've never been. Start by realizing you don't know the way. Read a travel guide: they tell you what to expect, and have maps—large maps of the whole country, maps of small neighborhoods you may visit along the way. A guide will tell you about local customs, how to say hello and ask for help. They give you warnings: what not to say, what to avoid. Study the language. Look at maps, gather any equipment you might need. Find someone to water the plants when you're gone.

With all this preparation, when we arrive in a place we have never been, perhaps with only a few words in the local language, we are a little lost and a little scared. We are dependent on strangers, relying on kindness and the fact that we are all more alike than different, and the hope that the people in this place will want to know us, too. We walk strange alleys and smell new scents and see a cast of light we've never seen before, across a landscape altogether new. Either we relax into this, trust, and look up, or we retreat and turn away. As you are walking the dog, doing the dishes, let your imagination go. What will it be like to go on this trip? What will it be like on the journey? Think about what you want to wear. Pack your bags.

I am comfortable talking about death, and often comfortable even with the fact of my own death, but I didn't get here in an unbroken line of good experiences. I began to practice Buddhism when I was filled with anxiety, almost agoraphobic. I have at times been really frightened of dying, frightened in an organic, shattering panic. I am comfortable now largely because of the time I've spent staring at it, touching it, thinking about it. Experience helps; there's no way around it. If you want to be more comfortable with death itself, with your death and the death of others, spend time near it. Read this travel guide and follow the maps and find a place where you can see what happens next—what will, like it or not, happen to you in time. One of the goals of my life is to become more congruent—less dissonant—and this is a religious journey to me. But this isn't a book of inspiration or spiritual guidance. I'm not going to tell you a lot of stories of lovely deaths or suggest meditations for a lonely night. There are plenty of books like that, but none will entirely console you. This isn't that kind of book. This is just a book about how you can get ready.

Carol and I used to scuba dive together. When I began to dive, I had a revelation: that I only feel wet when I am not completely submerged. Swimming on the surface, I am aware of water and air and the difference between them. I feel wet skin, splashing, damp hair. Underwater, I don't feel any of these things. "When the time comes for you to die, just die," the medieval Japanese master Dōgen wrote. "In death, there is nothing but death." What a mysterious phrase this is: "In death, there is nothing but death." What this means is that when we engage in anything completely, everything else disappears—not because we're concentrating on something else, not because we're looking away. Everything else disappears because it doesn't exist. This moment is all that exists. Just now is where we live. Life is completely life; death is completely death. Living or dying, this moment is everything if we submerge.

Carol was a great comic, and she would pose for me thirty feet below the surface of the sea. I can see her right now. She is floating weightlessly in clear water, lit by columns of sun. She pretends she is playing the piano. She pretends she is sleeping, curled up on her side like a cat. She pretends she is sitting in court, pounding her gavel. We laugh and laugh in this silly, free, perfect moment, and it is as though there is no water around us at all.

2

Resistance

It is a fine Thursday in September. My brother is visiting. We are about to go out for breakfast, when a friend from my Zen temple calls.

"What's up?" I ask as I pull on my shoes and look for my jacket. But his voice is serious; the words instantly fade out of reach. I hear only *Kyogen* and *heart attack* before I yelp. "What! No!" and then I am coping: "Okay, I'm coming, which hospital?" Kyogen has been my religious teacher for more than thirty years. For his birthday once, I gave him a small statue of Ganesha, a Hindu god who represents both removing and creating obstacles. Such is the nature of the challenging relationship between a religious teacher and a student. But deep, abiding love is part of it, too. He has been many things to me over the years, but as time passed, we became friends, traveling companions, and, finally, family.

Which hospital? I ask, because I am already on my way.

And then my friend says, *Wait.*

And then he says, *He died.*

No. I say it, or shout it, and then I find myself on the floor. *No.* When I look up, my brother is hovering beside me, confused. I try to explain, crying, gasping, even while I am ticking off the list of what I need to bring, even while a tsunami washes over me. *NO*. The dog? What should I do with the dog? My brother shifts from foot to foot: *What happened? Tell me what happened.* And then I just crumple and weep while he pats me awkwardly, saying, *Breathe*.

I get lost driving to a hospital I've been to many times before, park in the wrong lot, go to the wrong building, get lost twice more before I find the room. And when I walk in, I am walking into a new world where he lies in a hospital bed, so clearly himself and so clearly not alive. He is wearing a gown he would joke about if he could still joke. His wife sits in a chair beside him. She is crying; she has been crying for quite a while; I am crying, too, and it feels like I have been crying for hours. I love him more than my own hands. There is nothing to say, so I say, *Oh*. Oh. I think, *He died*, and the wave of disbelief breaks over me again. Decades of Zen practice, many hours at the bedsides of the dying, the loss of other people I loved—what these give me now is not acceptance but awareness of denial. A chance to not resist my resistance. To see my disbelief for what it is.

Other people arrive, and we bathe his limp, cooling body and dress him in a clean kimono. Several of us divide up a list of names and start making calls. I send urgent texts and leave voice messages telegraphing an unexplained disaster. I suddenly remember that tonight is a meeting of the death-and-dying study group I am leading, and I send an email to everyone to cancel the meeting.

In the vocabulary of grief, a grieving person has tasks: one must accept the reality of the death, feel its pain, adjust to the new world. But in the stark early hours and days, there are also chores. So many chores. I take on the funeral home. I call from the hallway, surrounded by visitors coming and going and sitting against the wall and pacing about. My chest feels as though it has been struck with a mallet, but I slide into the ordinary world again, where I say "Hello" and explain the situation and get put on hold and listen to bland music and then explain the special requirements—no embalming; a group to go into the crematorium and start the fire; the bones to be left alone—and get put on hold again and then agree on a price and say goodbye.

His body is in the last room on the cardiovascular unit, which is half-empty today. We fill the room and the hallway all day, supported by graceful, efficient nurses. One person after the other peeks in the unit's double doors: *Is this the place?* Some are crying, others look numb and barren. One marches straight into the room while another veers away, steps dragging. A few walk as though they are injured. In the room, people cry quietly or whisper and then lapse into silence. In the hallway, laughter and stories and hugs and more crying. There are people who cannot get away from work or must find a babysitter. One person is 150 miles away and begs us to wait, to keep the body there until she can reach us. We have forgotten to eat. A bereavement cart arrives with coffee and tea, and I buy cottage cheese and celery sticks and yogurt at the little café down the hall. We poke at everything. I go for a walk. Now and then a fog settles over me, a kind of numb confusion. Then another friend comes through the doors and we start over. We do this for fourteen hours.

Meanwhile, people come out of business meetings or the gym and return my calls. Bad news, I say, and begin to explain. They only hear "Kyogen" and "heart attack" before they yelp, *What? No!* and then, *Okay, I'm coming, which hospital?*

And I say, *Wait*.
And I say, *He died*.
No.

When I was in my thirties, I became afraid to fly. My life was complicated and demanding, but I was healthy. It was the kind of fear that had no rationale. Reading about the safety of flying didn't help; studying the causes of turbulence didn't make a difference. I talked to frequent flyers, to a counselor, and finally with a therapist who specialized in phobias. Nothing helped. I was simply very afraid whenever I was on a plane.

Fear of death begins in childhood. Children are sensitive to how adults talk about everything. With our hushed deflections and whispering, we can easily give children the message that death is not to be talked about at all, that silence is the only correct response. *Funerals are not for children.* Teenagers become acutely conscious of death, but they don't grasp its permanence—thus the near-constant risking of life that accompanies those years. Only as we mature into middle age does one's own death begin to seem real. My fear of flying was nothing more than a naked fear of dying—not in a plane crash, necessarily, but anywhere, ever. The Buddhist teacher Ken McLeod likes to ask his students to imagine all the ways they can die simply in going about their day. "Is there any circumstance that you can engage in in your life in which you're absolutely guaranteed of not dying?" he asks. There is not a single moment, a single place, where we are not in danger.

I couldn't articulate this for a while. I had come to the stark understanding that when I was flying I could not live without the airplane, that I was in a very dangerous situation. In time, I came to see that this danger was life's danger, the death I couldn't escape even on the ground. The safety of flying had nothing to do with it.

Now I can see that this fear appeared when it did precisely because this was a time when I was wielding strength and power. The fear was partly about being a parent and an adult in my own right—which is to say, I was afraid because I was growing and changing and time was passing. I had become aware of my own perishable nature—*mine*—which was nothing like anyone else's. It was *mine*. I was aware of all that I could lose—of all that, somewhere in the back part of my mind, I knew I would lose. A bumpy flight just reminded me in a way I couldn't avoid. It's a dangerous situation up there, just as it is down here, just as it is when I am doing the laundry or lying in bed half-asleep. As it always is.

I recently filled out several questionnaires intended to determine one's place on the actuarial tables. I'm doing okay. According to statistics, I have a less than 5 percent chance of dying within ten years. My blood pressure is excellent. My lipids and blood sugar are in a good range. My colonoscopy is clean. I've never smoked. I have about a 15 percent chance of developing breast cancer— almost double the normal rate, because of my mother's disease, but still low. My odds of dying in a car accident are low. My odds of dying in a plane crash are minuscule. But. But. I will die. I could die tomorrow. Tonight. (No I won't. Yes I will. No . . .)

The ancient Romans sometimes only said of a dead person, "*Vixit*"—"He has lived." The Laymi people of Bolivia say that a dead person has "gone to cultivate chili pepper." This could tell us, I suppose, that people have always avoided the subject. Most of the deaths in the program where I work come after a slow decline, telegraphed for weeks or months. In the last few weeks of life, the nurse often visits every day; she or he teaches the caregivers and the family what to expect, what symptoms mean, how to use medications, how to do everything possible to keep a person comfortable, and how to know when death is imminent. And yet that same nurse may chart that a person has *passed away*. She is *deceased,* she has *expired*. Sometimes the nurse cannot bring herself to write the bare, undeniable word.

All the fears we don't say out loud. Never speaking about it at all, we come to believe that others don't feel as we do. That somehow every other person in the world is at ease in their own skin, and I am the only imposter. But of course this is nonsense. Everyone has moments of feeling adult life is out of their reach: the responsibilities, the demands. The death at the end. How long will dying take? Will it hurt? What if I can't breathe? Will I say something embarrassing? What if I'm alone? What if I'm with others? *Will it hurt?* What if no one notices? We fear what comes after the last moment. You have your own questions for that.

In her book *Talking About Death Won't Kill You,* Virginia Morris, a journalist, has made a long list of fears collected from interviews. Fear of having an autopsy, having the body mutilated or taken apart—fairly common. People are afraid of being ignored when they are dying, or of being abandoned by their family. We are afraid that we will be ugly. We fear that there is no heaven. We fear there is a heaven and we won't be allowed to enter. People worry about what it will be like to be weak and dependent. They fear having others make decisions for them, having no modesty, losing their privacy. We fear leaving something undone: work, a

project, a story. (This book.) Many people fear becoming a burden to their family, that their lingering deaths will impoverish a
spouse and ruin a child's health. You may be afraid of dying in
your sleep. You may be afraid of dying when you are awake. A
person who has watched the long diminishing of a parent fears
nothing more than his own diminishment.

Do you feel guilty about being afraid to die? Do you think
you should have more equanimity? Perhaps you are a little su-
perstitious. Don't tell anyone—don't ever admit it—but maybe
you have just a little sense of being complicit, of making it come
true. When my mother was dying and I said so, *right out loud*,
my grandmother hissed at me like a snake. She believed that
one could cause a person to die this way. You may be afraid of
dying suddenly or afraid of dying slowly. People fear that they
will lose control and cry or shout or curse. People fear that others will watch and judge them if they lose control. (People fear
being watched all the time.) You may fear that no one will miss
you. You may fear, more than anything, losing your hair. Or
being on a ventilator. Or needles—a lot of people fear needles.
Some people fear pain: pain, pain is what they think about, pain
is what they dread. Another person can think only of struggling
to breathe, and another of soiling the bed, anything but that.
You may fear that you will wake up in the coffin; many people
fear this. Perhaps you are afraid that the all-pervading quality of
being dead is loneliness.

Morris's particular fear is that she has no idea when it will
happen and thus is always on edge. Always waiting. "Do you have
thirty years left, or just a few days?" We may see death coming
from far away, like a train while we stand at the platform and
check our watches. We may see death all at once, in the flash

of headlights or a stopped heart. We may wake up right in the middle of it, like a dream.

My friend, the poet Steve Tyler, has had a dodgy heart for years now: its beats are irregular, often too slow. He lives alone with his dog, and when he worries about dying, sometimes he worries that his dog will be trapped in the house. These are the things we worry about but rarely say aloud. In Steve's lovely poem "Heart Fading," he describes the feeling when his heart slows down and he grows faint, his mind fading like "the radio of a car / driving further and further away from the station." When that happens, he goes outside and sits on the porch. That way, if he dies, if his heart leads him into the "white noise / Between stations," his neighbors or the mail carrier will find him and rescue his dog.

The legal scholar Louise Harmon notes that we don't really confront our own real deaths except "in the dark, in the damp-ness of Aristotelian sweat." To accept death is to accept that this body belongs to the world. This body is subject to all the forces in the world. This body can be broken. This body will run down. "Golden lads and girls all must, / As chimney-sweepers, come to dust." (Except, maybe, me.) I lean a little on the words of oth-ers, but I don't want to forget that quotes and poems are com-posed words, reflections formed beside the fire when nothing was breathing down Cicero's neck. But what about that moment when you step firmly off the curb and hear the shrieking brakes behind you? When you are alone at home and a knife seems to shoot through your chest? What about that day in the exam room when your bare feet are dangling off the table and you've just heard the diagnosis and are trying not to cry? We may not sit down to discuss our wishes and fears until it is almost—and sometimes truly is—too late. I may believe it is true that contemplating death makes life ever sweeter. But I also believe you are not thinking this when the person you love is gasping for a final breath. Then all the world's philosophy turns to vapor and the only prayer you can remember is *Please*. No words help and no one else's death counts.

I am fond of a story I heard about Dainin Katagiri, the Buddhist teacher I quoted in the first chapter. When he was still a young man, his teacher, Shunryu Suzuki, was dying. All the major disciples were sitting around the deathbed in silence, meditating, when Katagiri arrived. He flung himself into the room, crying out, "Don't die!" I don't know if this story is true. We should never ask people not to die, but I am touched by this image of authenticity. Katagiri, the Zen priest, the model of decorum, couldn't care less what others thought of him in that moment.

At some point, most of us shift from realizing that sooner or later some future self will die to realizing that *this very self*, me, precious and irreplaceable me, will die. It's a terrible thing to grasp, and though this insight may last a mere second, it changes your life. To know that the physical body will cease to exist at some point—that *this* life will end   changes us. I've felt this knowledge like an electric shock and also as a kind of honeyed happiness. For an instant now and then, I've had the beauty of the china bowl right here in my hands.

Poor Elisabeth Kübler-Ross: so misunderstood. She is widely credited with identifying the five stages of grief. She didn't. Kübler-Ross worked with dying people, not grieving people. She identified clear phases people go through when they are dying not as stages but as emotional experiences that come and go and may overlap. Decades after her research, I routinely come across references to the "five stages of grief." People grieving a loss are surprised to find they are not traversing through the expected "five stages" in a straightforward way. It's all more complicated than that.

In 1969, Kübler-Ross was working as a psychiatrist. She often encountered doctors who left orders not to tell a patient how sick they were. Doctors lied to patients about their prognosis or evaded the truth when asked. So she began to interview patients about what they knew and wanted.

Her book *On Death and Dying* is a plain summary of narrative research she did into the coping mechanisms of people with a terminal illness. The coping mechanisms of the dying person, she decided, could be described as denial and isolation, anger (which includes "rage, envy, and resentment"), bargaining (which means "entering into some sort of an agreement which may postpone the inevitable happening"), depression ("a sense of great loss"), and acceptance (in which the person is "neither depressed nor angry about his 'fate'" but instead feels "a certain degree of quiet expectation"). Kübler-Ross saw these states as "defense mechanisms in psychiatric terms, coping mechanisms to deal with extremely difficult situations. These means will last for different periods of time and will replace each other or exist at times side by side." She was a psychiatrist, after all.

Kübler-Ross found that many doctors and nurses claimed the actively dying patient didn't need their care, and withdrew from the bedside. Others resented the dying for wasting their time. "I am convinced," she wrote, "that those doctors who need denial themselves will find it in their patients." The most important task in taking care of the dying, she realized, is to deal with your own fears.

Experience helps: I have been forced to believe in my own death over and over again. And yet I get distracted. I resist. I forget. I am reminded again; I believe again. Of course people die. Everyone dies. Except (secretly, without the conscious thought) me. Such internal contradiction, these emotional and cognitive dissonances, are the complications that make us human and difficult and fascinating. I say yes and I say no; I am scared and I am curious; I refuse and I accept.

Epicurus, one of those philosophers we like to cite when we talk about death, was a Greek who founded a school of simple living and deep reflection. Epicurus thought the fundamental source of human anguish is the fear of death. He developed thought experiments to illustrate that the fear of annihilation is illogical: if you're extinguished, you can't regret extinction. There's nothing to fear about nothing. In nothingness, there is no perception, no consciousness, no memory. "That most fearful of all bad things, death, is nothing to us, since when we are, death has not come, and when death is present, we are not." (Many centuries later, Bernard de Fontenelle echoed him. He was a month short of a hundred years old when he died, saying, "I feel nothing except a certain difficulty in continuing to exist.")

Epicurus died at the age of seventy-two from prostatitis, which he found a misery.

His attempt at comforting words fails to comfort many people. The idea that there will come a time when *I am not* is exactly what we fear. The Internet is a handy place to express and fuel our fears; there are many forums available for people who are afraid of dying. One woman writes of this particular ache: "I just think it's such a horrible thought to completely cease to exist, everything we have ever known, every thought i have ever had, every person that i have ever loved or valued just gone, gone for all of eternity. I can barely think about it the thought is so distressing." The psychiatrist Irvin Yalom describes the ego facing extinction as being "staggered by the enormity of eternity, of being dead forever and ever and ever and ever." I like that repetition. Ever and ever and ever. Exactly.

I was interested to hear about a recent study in *Psychological Science* showing that contemplating one's death makes you happier. The researchers asked people either to contemplate death or to contemplate dental pain. Then people were given combinations of letters and asked to fill in a word. For instance, *an* might become *angry* or *angle*; *jo* could be *joy* or *job*; and so on. The researchers found that those who had been contemplating death made significantly more positive choices of words than those contemplating a bad tooth.

That's more like it, I thought. At last, a confirmation of a kind, that knowing we are going to die is not a terrible thing. But when I read more of the study, I saw the bias of the researchers, who didn't think the results meant what I thought they meant. One said in an interview, "We are all walking around, unlike every other animal, thinking, 'Oh, my God, eventually this all ends.'" Why would that make us happier? Because, they wrote, considering death evokes a psychological "immune response." We cope with our distress by subconsciously invoking happier sensations, because otherwise we would be paralyzed by despair.

The researchers' conclusion derives from the psychological idea known as terror management theory. I just love that phrase; talk about hubris. TMT is a complicated idea and not without controversy, but aspects of this idea have been the subject of hundreds of studies. TMT even has its own vocabulary: to be aware of our impending death is "mortality salience."

Terror management theory has a deep pedigree. Our cultural

shift to a scientific view was long and painful and part of a vast cultural change in how the world and human life and death was viewed. "The skull will grin in at the banquet," in the words of William James, who wrote at length about the divided self: the stoic and the passionate, the aware and the repressed selves. He noted the type of personality he called "healthy-minded," of which he was a bit suspicious, "with its strange power of living in the moment and ignoring and forgetting." The rest, the "sick souls" (of whom he was one), can't hide from the fact of mortality and all it implies. To secular thinkers like Darwin and Freud, death was a principle of life. How could we reconcile the polarities of experience? Death was both unnatural—unbidden, undesired, caused by uncontrollable outside forces—and completely natural, because everything dies. "It was not life after death that Darwin and Freud speculated about, but life with death," writes the psychotherapist Adam Phillips of the two. "What else could a life be now but a grief-stricken project?" How does the inquisitive human mind cope with its inevitable deconstruction? In this view, death is not natural even to the dying person. It is an assault.

The psychoanalyst Otto Rank paired "life anxiety" and "death anxiety." He called the first that of realizing one's self as an individual, one who is vulnerable, lonely, separate. The latter is the realization that the only way to overcome our loneliness is to merge with others and lose our precious individuality. We are left afraid of both life and death. In 1973, Ernest Becker, a cultural anthropologist, built on the ideas of Rank and others in an influential book called *The Denial of Death*. He believed that the "fear-of-death layer" is innermost in the human psyche, "the layer of our true and basic animal anxieties, the terror that we carry around in our secret heart." The human, he wrote, "is a worm and food for worms . . . a terrifying dilemma to be in and to have to live with."

Becker thought that the human being is the only animal both aware of its inevitable death and aware of its animal life. And humans are terrified of their animal lives. This dissonance is what really makes us unique. We live in and participate in an ecosystem of death, in which everything is eating and being eaten. But the human creature, obsessed with its inner life, also perceives the vastness of the universe. Humans know past and future as well as now. We can imagine the beginning of the galaxy and the death of the sun. Becker believed that this awareness of our small and temporary existence in a seemingly infinite space is our real problem. Humans know they have a flimsy body, limited in time, and this body is "a *problem* to him that has to be explained"—a body that changes and has memories and dreams and eventually disappears. The human cannot abide the thought of death and can hardly bear being alive.

Most people aren't wrestling with dread so much as trying to ignore a chronic background anxiety. But Becker would say this is just repression. He believed that we succeed so well at repressing the fear of death that we may deny the fear even exists—yet its energy remains, driving us on to create a network of belief and relationship in which our short, fragile lives will have meaning. We call these networks by various names: philosophy, but also psychology, science, culture, religion, and art. Repressed, anxious but refusing to experience the anxiety completely, humans create civilization.

To contemplate death, as is done in many religions, is to invite Becker's terror. But for many people, the result is a kind of liberation. An entire tradition of painting in Japan, *kusōzu*, was devoted to portraying the nine stages of a decaying corpse. The churches of Europe are draped with the carvings of skeletons. In Christian terms: "We must all die; we are like water spilt on the ground, which cannot be gathered up again." Muslims are encouraged to contemplate death regularly. The Buddha sent many of his disciples to the charnel ground to do what came to be called corpse meditation. He outlined the specific kind of corpse a person should meditate upon, depending on their need. A person who lusts after a beautiful figure should meditate on a swollen corpse. A person who is vain about their fine complexion should meditate on a discolored corpse. One of the meditations goes like this: "Verily, exactly so is also my own body. It is of the same nature! Just so will this body become disgusting and it can never escape this fate!" This is medicine for pride but also for the false belief that we can escape change. When he was himself dying, the Buddha lay on the ground in front of everyone, saying, "Don't look away." Saying, "You, too, will be like this."

In Michel de Montaigne's words, "We make the cure harder precisely because we do not realize we are ill." Montaigne thought about death often. He was an erudite, skeptical man, and he wrote of intimate matters during a time of great social upheaval. He essentially created the personal essay by turning his glass on himself when everyone else was looking outward. "Let us deprive death of its strangeness," he wrote. "Let us frequent it, let us get used to it." Think often of death and get on with life, Montaigne wrote. "I want Death to find me planting my cabbages, neither worrying about it nor the unfinished gardening."

Virginia Morris suggests that you brace yourself. I like that phrase. *Brace yourself.* Name your fears, she says, and then names

those fears, every fear she can imagine. Name each one, no matter how irrational. Rehearse the crisis like a soldier or surgeon
who acts out what to do so that nothing is a complete surprise.
I particularly like her way of describing death, considering how
I've gotten here: "We all know for a fact that we are headed for a
crash," she writes. "We have to accept that the crash will happen."
So, imagine the crash. Imagine it in all its permutations.

We are seeing the beginning of what is often called a death
awareness movement. (Of course, like eating fresh vegetables and
being awake during childbirth, awareness of death is just something
old made new again.) Death Cafes began in the United Kingdom
in 2011. At a Death Cafe, small groups of people come together
in a casual setting to discuss death in any way they choose. Death
Cafes are a "social franchise," available to anyone willing to follow
the guidelines: not-for-profit, promoting no particular point of
view, and confidential. Several thousand have taken place in fifty-
one countries so far.

Death Salon is a different beast: the name is trademarked. It
has a professional staff and holds large, ticketed public events.
There are scientific lectures and symposiums on everything from
pioneer graveyards and Ghanaian coffin makers to the use of CT
scans in autopsies and an exhibit of "skin books" (which are just
what you think they are). Death Salon is sponsored by a group
called the Order of the Good Death. Its founding members are
funeral industry professionals, artists, and academics. They are
mostly white, mostly young, and aggressively hip with supposed
professions like "postmortem jewelry designer," "morbid cake
maker," and "international corpse explorer."

YouTube has entire channels devoted to dead bodies. The
Nourishing Death blog, about the cultural relationship between

death and food, will help you decide what you should make for your aunt's funeral reception. If you're interested in skin books, you can go to the Anthropodermic Book Project page. But why would we mistake an abundance of information for peace of mind? The official mission statement of the Order of the Good Death describes "making death a part of your life. Staring down your death fears—whether it be your own death, the death of those you love, the pain of dying, the afterlife (or lack thereof), grief, corpses, bodily decomposition, or all of the above. Accepting that death itself is natural, but the death anxiety of modern culture is not."

Perhaps we can call this a movement; I'm not convinced. I think anxiety about death is a part of being human—Cicero and Darwin and all that. Do we know of a single culture in human history that has not had rituals to manage death and the fear of death? Hiding death isn't universal; worrying about death may be. Does all this sharing among strangers help? No matter how bluntly presented, death on the lecture circuit is theoretical, and a lot of comments on the Web don't form a conversation. As long as we have to go to a lecture to see a corpse or meet with strangers in a coffee shop in order to talk about our most intimate of moments, there's something vital missing. It doesn't matter if you can attend a lecture on Civil War surgical techniques if you can't talk to your doctor about your own death.

I am not afraid of dying—that is, I don't feel afraid to be a dying person, weak, sick. Sometimes I am curious. I am comforted by having seen peaceful deaths. But my curiosity about dying is the calm, sitting-by-the-fire kind. I do so want to keep on living and living and living. I can imagine being a dying person, but I still find it hard to believe that someday I will be dead. You, yes: you will die. But I—well, I don't really believe that. Such hubris. But how can we let go of our lives? It's impossible that you will leave me and even more impossible that I won't exist. We walk around with a blinkered, partial denial of death. Yes, we will die, but not now, not here. This dissonance is strong and strange—to absolutely know this will happen, and against all evidence to the contrary, to absolutely not know. (It's so hard to believe. When the Buddha's own death was imminent, his closest followers wept and flung themselves on the ground and cried in lament: "Too soon!") I understand bargaining. I've tried to make a lot of deals with the universe, and this is one: I'm ready to die *if*—I'm ready to die *when*. Just not now.

Acceptance is found only by wholly inhabiting our denial. Contemplating death is really contemplating resistance, and for a long time. How do we get ready to die? We start with not being ready. We start with the fact that we are afraid. A long, lonesome examination of our fear. We start by admitting that we are all future corpses pretending we don't know.

I fly comfortably most of the time now. I rarely take prescription drugs anymore. I usually choose a window seat. I walk down to the plane, take my seat, settle in with a book. But I put down the book when the plane accelerates and attend to what is happening. I feel the speed, the lift. I feel the wheels separate from the ground and try to give myself over to the plane's life. Often I gaze out the window, watching clouds, shadows, light. My personal belief is that physical death is a painless dissolution of the separate self, that our true nature is spacious and unbounded. But now and then, when the plane slips and stumbles over the clouds, my racing heart returns. The organism reacts.

Usually I feel the plane leave the ground and rise into the air and I look out the window at the vast and mostly empty, inhuman world and I think, *This plane is my body. This air, this water, this earth, is my body.* And in a way that has nothing to do with religion or faith or belief in what comes next: *This body is me.* And it will someday cease to be at all.

3

A Good Death

Almost two-thirds of adults in the United States believe that it's reasonable to allow a person to die sometimes. People say that living as long as possible is easily the least important aspect of facing death. They define a good death as one free of pain, peaceful, and calm. A good death includes family and friends, and a chance to reflect on one's life. The federal government (in the guise of its Health and Medicine Division of the National Academies of Sciences, Engineering, and Medicine) says that a good death is "one free from avoidable distress and suffering for patients, families and caregivers; in general accord with patients' and families' wishes and reasonably consistent with clinical, cultural and ethical standards." But what does any of that mean? Do we want to be pain-free if it means we will be sleeping much of the time? Do we want someone with us all the time, or do we want times of solitude? What if a patient's wishes conflict with a family's hopes, or with a clinical standard? A quiet death is not necessarily a good death. A person may be quiet and filled with emotional anguish. A noisy death is not necessarily a bad one; periods of restlessness and delirium are common with dying. Most people have loud breathing in their last hours or days but seem undisturbed by it. (I will discuss these symptoms in more detail in later chapters.)

It can be a noisy, even fearsome struggle to be born. There may be moments of fierceness when we die. Ira Byock, a hospice physician, says that it can be "like an animal shedding its skin, a physical struggle to wriggle out of this life." A grief specialist compares dying to the efforts of a butterfly to break out of its cocoon. Elisabeth Kübler-Ross called the moment of death the "silence that goes beyond words." But that moment may not be quiet.

As we examine our expectations about death, we invariably diverge from each other. If we are too focused on a specific experience—that meadow, the scent of baking bread, whether Aunt Lois will get here in time—we are presuming a degree of control that may not be possible. Rather than defining what a good death looks like, we are better off thinking about what surrounds death as it is.

Better to speak instead about how the conditions of dying are supported. We can allow a dying person to make what choices are possible, accepting that these choices may be few and may have been made months or years before, or may in fact be made by a proxy. We can see that the person is spoken to, not about, even while acknowledging that the person may not be awake. We can treat symptoms, but only to support what the dying person wants. The person in bed leads the way, and may lead the way from words written far in the past, or from conversations with relatives, or from what is known or guessed about what this person wants. The family members and caregivers can be careful not to impose their own beliefs. This is what Virginia Morris deemed "a death unhidden, a death reclaimed." Such a death can take many shapes.

Perry was a veteran who had been homeless for years at a time. He was also a hunter and comfortable in the wilderness. When he was diagnosed with terminal cancer, he said that he wanted to "die like an animal." That phrase is one of despair to most of us, but to Perry, life as an animal made real sense. It meant dying in the most natural way, the way a deer or bear would die: alone, silent, close to the ground.

He was not strong enough to get to the forest, so he had to die in his apartment. He refused almost all medications, including anything for pain—and he had pain, sometimes a lot. He wanted to feel it, he said. He wanted to be awake to what was happening, to all of it. In his last weeks, like most dying people, he took very little food or water. But he also refused help with most of his personal needs. He didn't want to be changed when he lost control of his bladder and bowels. He didn't want to be bathed. That was what death meant to Perry: the failing of the body, the slow dissolution and breakdown of life into its component parts, which is a messy thing.

Perry's choice of how to die was distressing to most of his caregivers. He was not without support—quite the opposite. He didn't have family, but he had a doctor, a visiting nurse, a social worker, a chaplain, and a team of nurse's aides who stayed with him for much of the day and night, though he often refused their assistance. Most of his caregivers simply kept trying—trying to help Perry bathe, talk, to change his linens, to give him a little pain medication or water if he would accept it.

Several people on the home care team asked the ethics committee to review Perry's death. I was in the group that felt he clearly had the capacity to make decisions. He had in fact calmly made his wishes clear again and again. I could accept his choice by framing it as one of personal power: the right of people to make their own choices, even bad ones, even self-destructive ones. The right to lead the way, even if that way was contrary to what everyone around him wanted. And, of course, this reveals something about me, about my biases and my own desires.

In the West, the earliest mortality charts are from the seventeenth century. It had long been believed that God defined the length of a life. Almost everyone died of accidents or infectious disease, so many people died sooner than the presumed limit. But no one could live longer. The length of life and the kind of death for each was written in a divine hand, and one's death was a good indication of what was going to happen afterward. (Pity the fellow who died in a fire.)

As scientists began to understand human biology, beliefs changed. Deaths from infectious diseases, accidents, and behavior—what we might today call lifestyle choices—all came to be seen as preventable, not divinely dictated. Today, most people in the United States die of chronic illness such as heart disease, cancer, respiratory disease, and diabetes. A great deal of money is being spent to change this fact—that is, to try to make all these things even more preventable, to push death back, though we have only compromised agreements for when death happens.

Kyogen used to say to me, "I'm not afraid to die. I'm just not ready." He always had something ahead, always more projects and plans. He wanted to write another book. He wanted to see Vienna. How did he feel that morning, stumbling down the street by himself, the chest pain like a train collision, until he slumped under a tree? How did he feel, alone on the sidewalk under a tree in the early morning, struggling to open a brand-new bottle of nitroglycerin tablets? Did he have a bitter moment or two as he waited for help? Did he know what was coming? In the crush of paramedics, the shouting, the needles, the ambulance racing, the sirens, when his shirt was ripped open for the sticky EKG pads, during the violence of what we call advanced cardiac life support, what was he feeling? Was he aware? In the long minutes of chest pounding and shock, did he know? Or was he already gone? At what point did he nod his head and say: *All right.* Having known him for so long, I can believe that he accepted it, that he was not afraid, that he let go when he knew it was time—and perhaps this letting go is why resuscitation doesn't work most of the time. I can believe this, but I don't know *when* he died.

Each of the obvious signs of death—not breathing, the heart stopping, the body turning cold—can all happen without a person dying. Respiratory failure can happen, as in a drowning, without stopping the heart. The heart can stop and start again or go into a wild arrhythmia without affecting respiration. A hypothermia victim may appear dead, their skin cold and muscles stiff. All of these conditions can be reversed. Is death the unbecoming of a person, the disintegration of a person's wholeness, which may precede organic death by years? The transformation, life to death, alive to dead, is unknowable. All we can do is choose. The traditional *cardiopulmonary standard* declares that death is the *irreversible cessation of cardiopulmonary function.* A person is declared dead from respiratory and cardiac failure only when they have had no heartbeat and have not been spontaneously breathing for some time. Is a person actually dead during resuscitation, when the vital functions are being produced from outside, through CPR and shock? We say no; he is not dead until the effort to revive him is over. (You're dead when the team says you're dead.)

We may describe death as the cessation of the body's sole function, which is staying alive—define it as the moment when the biological processes that prevent decomposition cease. How we define *death* depends on the direction we are facing. One approach, known as whole brain, states that *human death is the irreversible cessation of functioning of the entire brain, including the brain stem.* The higher-brain approach states that *human death is the irreversible cessation of the capacity for consciousness.* Loss of the functioning brain eventually kills the heart, and loss of the heart eventually kills the brain, and loss of breathing kills both. But at what point is selfhood lost?

The lawyer Louise Harmon, in her book, *Fragments on the Deathwatch*, explores the ramifications of how we define the declaration of death. She believes the central question is not "How do we define death?" but "When is it morally justifiable to treat a person as dead?" Considering the definition of *death* requires us to consider the definition of *life*, and that requires us to consider the meaning of *human being.*

The bioethicist Baruch Brody suggests that people are either alive, dead, or in a condition "during which they do not fully belong to either. . . . Death is a fuzzy set." There are philosophers who claim that the boundaries of death are actually so vague that it is not really possible to define it. (In summarizing the broad implications of a world without a precise definition of *death*, philosopher David DeGrazia writes, "Society may then select, among admissible standards, whichever is most attractive for practical purposes." The very definition of *slippery slope*.)

*   *   *

Most people say a good death is *timely*. But this is not a word we all define the same way. At what age is it time to die? We assume that a good life must be a long life. But I have seen some really bad long lives, and known happy, fulfilled people who lived fairly short ones. The quality of a life doesn't depend on its length; we aren't promised anything when we get here.

"What madness it is to expect to die of that failing of our powers brought on by extreme old age," wrote Montaigne, poking about in his cabbages. "We call that death, alone, a natural death, as if it were unnatural to find a man breaking his neck in a fall, engulfed in a shipwreck, surprised by a plague or pleurisy," he wrote. He was forty-seven then, a retired lawyer living in the country, already an old man for his time. "[P]erhaps we ought, rather, to call natural anything which is generic, common to all and universal." Montaigne died twelve years later, of inflamed tonsils.

While we may have the great good luck to live with antibiotics, vaccinations, and mandatory seat belt laws, people still break their necks. People drown; plagues abound. We can be angry about lousy lifestyle choices or a lack of primary health care or the costs of good nursing at the end of our lives and still see that death is natural. If someone dies suddenly, is it a bad death? Even with the best of care, people have heart attacks and strokes. People do fall down and crack their heads open. Death is a literal part of our nature. We can be angry about our nature, but it won't get us very far.

Early spring. I am sitting on the couch beside the napping dog, late at night. I hear a short, loud thud, the sound of a large appliance falling over. A boxed appliance. I pull the blinds and can see a motorcycle parked on the corner. A woman stands beside it, looking up the street. The hedge hides what she sees. I leave the dog and go outside. A neighbor, wearing pajamas, walks past. "You heard that?" he asks.

I walk around the hedge and see a small, ruined car, sideways in the center of the street. The front end is battered flat, the rear tires ruptured into strips, a white air bag filling the front seat. A man stands beside the open driver's door. There is another man lying on the pavement near me. He is wearing a motorcycle helmet, and from beneath it glides a slow syrup of blood. He is unmoving, arms thrown out. A mangled motorcycle lies across his lower legs.

A young man kneels at his head, cradling the helmet. Many people mill about, but he is the only one near this man. I kneel on the other side. Now I can see the gray pallor of the face, the eyes fixed, half-open, the small pool of dark blood that is not growing anymore. He is a big guy. The young man says, "We have to stabilize his neck." He is quiet a moment, then adds, "I don't think he's breathing."

"Is he okay? Oh my god, oh my god," a tall man standing nearby says, his voice tight. He is wearing a white leather biker's jacket and holding a motorcycle helmet.

I feel for a pulse in the thick neck and my knees roll across street grit. I look up at a woman nearby and ask if she's called 911. She nods.

The man beside me is very young. "Come back to us, dude," he murmurs, "come back," bending his own head close to the man's face.

"He's not breathing," I say. "There's no pulse."

"We can't take the helmet off," he says, and I hear his stress and I feel my stress, the tight, timeless tension. "We have to stabilize his *neck*," he says, and I want to say and perhaps I do say, *This guy is dead, his neck is not the problem*—but the young man is shaking his head, pleading with me. I look around, at a crowd of people staring, bright headlights from odd directions. *Why aren't I hearing sirens?* The firehouse is only a few blocks away.

The tall man says, "He's my roommate," stepping back and forth, back and forth, like a bird. "That's my bike," he tells me, waving at the motorcycle on the corner. He is beginning to realize this isn't just a bad spill.

I begin compressions, and there is a strange mushy sensation, ribs crushed, and something more, the startling absence; it feels like flicking a familiar light switch and nothing happens and you flick it again, and again, because light is what you expect. Now I'm thinking about vital organs and oxygenation and maybe paramedics in a minute or two who can intubate and shock, because maybe this guy has a heart that wants to beat again long enough to give away a kidney or two. I do it because the sweet young man is still whispering, "Come back to us, dude," and because a lot of people are watching as though waiting for a play to begin.

These compressions I am doing—counting, the way we are taught to do, by singing to myself, *Stayin' alive, stayin' alive,* and damn, if John Travolta's magic swaying walk down the sidewalk doesn't come to mind—these are bad compressions. I'm not really trying. This is crappy, pointless. Too many minutes have passed. They passed before I even strolled out of my apartment. Too many minutes without oxygen. But almost because of that, the futility, because *I can do better than this,* because his chest is soft and his limbs are flaccid and there is no life in this man, I renew my efforts. Then a skinny guy who looks too young to drink kneels beside me; he is holding a stethoscope. "I'm a doctor," he says, and I sit back on my heels so he can listen. He sees what I see, the gray skin, the unmoving puddle of blood, and says, with the same reluctance I'm feeling, "Do you want me to take over?"

"No," I say. "I'm fine." And I don't start again.

And there are the lights at last, the red and blue, the burly guys in firefighter turnouts carrying heavy boxes. The rest of us step aside, but their practiced eyes take it in and they aren't moving very fast. A firefighter shakes out a shiny silver blanket and drapes it over the man on the ground.

Maybe your vision of a good death is Grandpa at home in bed, surrounded by his loving family, whispering "I love you" to each person in turn. (One of my favorite cartoons shows a scene like this, and the person in bed is saying, "These are my last words. No, wait—*these* are my last words. No, wait . . .") Such a death is uncommon. People dying slowly of a chronic illness also die suddenly from such things as a seizure or hemorrhage, and if they don't, they are likely not talking. Almost everyone who dies slowly from illness or age is unconscious in the last hours or days—or at least silent. Is a dying person who appears to be unconscious in the same state as a person who has fainted? Or a person who is sleeping?

Whatever the state is, many people are not responsive when they die. Their eyes are closed or even fixed; they don't seem to be aware of others. They are quiet, and so we call it peaceful, but how do we know? A person who does not seem to be awake may be conscious in a way we don't grasp. They may be paying very close attention to what is happening right now. They may be whispering "I love you" in a voice you cannot hear. I don't know. No one knows. Maybe, like a lot of people, you imagine that the best death is the one that steals upon us in our sleep. That seems sudden to me.

The fantasy of a quiet leave-taking in complete control is, for the most part, just that. A fantasy. Our ideals about the so-called good death are constricting. Death is not something at which we succeed or fail, something to achieve. Life and death are not possessions. If we think it has to look a certain way, do we judge anything else as lacking? Be wary of the leap to disapproval about what a person says he or she wants or has planned. We die in breathtaking solitude. The value of a death doesn't depend on what anyone else thinks about it. My death belongs only to me; its value is known only by me. Can our death fit our life? Can it reflect the way we have tried to live, wanted to live? Rather than glibly wishing for a "good death," perhaps we are better off thinking of a "fitting death."

Common definitions of a good death also presume that the dying person is accepting of his fate, preferably in a way clearly visible to others. In the government's definition of this singular event, did you notice the unapologetic inclusion of others? Most definitions of a good death are social at the core, counting the experience of caregivers, family, and witnesses as part of the event. You may be fine, but if your uncle Phil or your nurse's aide is unhappy—well, maybe we should fix that.

One of the witnesses to a death is the institution surrounding it. A study of how hospices defined a good death concluded that it requires a "socially responsible individual who quietly slips away once all that could be done is seen to have been done." It's hard for the caregiver and witnesses to be at ease if they think the dying person is not at ease, or is not behaving as expected, or is not asking for what they assume he or she must want. These demands can be stifling during an event that is, in fact, invisible to all but one. This can very easily become a subtle form of coercion, the family and caregivers ever so gently bearing down upon the patient to express readiness, to behave in certain ways and say the right words whether they mean them or not. This ensures that the family and caregivers get the good death they desire. And all these nonpatient others are assumed to agree on everything: family members won't argue about treatment or act out old scripts in the hallway late at night or try to play nurses and doctors off each other.

A hospice unit in particular has a vested interest in providing visibly "good" deaths. The stories of these good deaths are told again and again. The staff reassures families and patients with examples of people who made fond farewells, sorted out the family photographs, met with a minister regularly, and played the ukulele for everyone. Those who don't fit this picture are problematic. They become case studies instead.

One of the most common fears people express about death is that of losing one's dignity. Sir Thomas Browne wrote that he was "not so much afraid of death, as ashamed thereof; 'tis the very disgrace and ignominy of our natures, that in a moment can so disfigure us, that our nearest friends, Wife, and Children stand afraid and start at us." Browne so hated the idea of the "teares of pity" that accompanied death that he wished to be drowned instead, where no one could see.

Loss of dignity is one of the most common reasons people give for choosing assisted death, and we refer to assisted death with the prettified phrase *death with dignity*. Death is dignified only because you choose it. One man dreads "all of those painful and demeaning things" that come from being dependent for his care; another person fears having to be fed, and another needing to be helped to the bathroom. Such things feel *below our dignity* somehow, though we may lovingly do such things for each other without concern.

We have a deep need for autonomy. The concept of human rights is based on the idea that humans have an inherent dignity by virtue of being human. Refugees and prisoners of war deserve our help because they have intrinsic worth; they deserve to be treated well because they are human. But we also say of refugees and prisoners of war that they are suffering an "indignity" because they are unable to make choices for themselves. Which is it? Are we always creatures of dignity because of our core quality? Or does our quality depend on our control?

We know that serious illness means we will need help, that illness is a visible state and privacy is largely sacrificed. Many people will describe how important it was to be the caregiver for another, what a humbling experience it was to do for another when the person was too weak to do for himself. Perhaps you will vigorously deny that physical weakness is undignified in and of itself. After all, everyone cries sometimes; everyone needs help. But this is one of our favorite double standards. It's all right for you to cry; of course, you need to cry. It's okay for my elderly grandmother to need help going to the bathroom. But I won't let you see me cry. I won't let you help *me* to the bathroom. That's different.

Ruthann Robson has a rare cancer. "Someone actually tells me this," she writes. "'I really admire the way you are conducting yourself with such dignity.'" Robson demurs. She is crying in the bathroom at work, puking in the evening at home. Her hair has fallen out. She is so tired she can barely stand. The woman seems to see Robson's behavior as dignified because all this desperation is taking place behind closed doors. Because she seems to be *in control*. How often do we read obituaries praising the deceased for their "brave battle" and "heroic fight," for "never complaining," for "remaining dignified throughout her illness"? We value the stoic exterior; it spares the witnesses. Of course, a quiet demeanor may mask emotional distress; agitation may be a small wave over an ocean of calm. We like distress to stay hidden, to not make us uncomfortable. We want death to *look* nice as much as to feel nice. Do you have the urge to make death special? Transcendent, spiritual? Death is often a little messy; what happens then? Robson adds, "When I look at her, I see my dying reflected back to me, a shiny silvery object without form or function, an abyss of pity." No emotion creates more distance between us than pity. We are human and sometimes we cry. Sometimes we lose our tempers, tremble with fear, puke, and wet our pants. This is life; this is death.

If dignity arises from our inherent worth, then aging, illness, and weakness can't affect it. We can be upright even while falling down. I think one of the marks of maturity—at least, a marker I have been working on my entire adult life—is the willingness to be seen exactly as I am. As we grow more settled and mature, we become less hidden to others, more transparent to ourselves as well as to each other. With this growing authenticity comes a deepening of intimacy with each other. We are no longer appearances banging against each other but real people looking at each other. Authenticity and intimacy go together; intimacy and loss go together. You can't have one without the other. Knowing one's self makes it possible to be seen by others, and makes it possible to see each other, however we are. Broken, vulnerable, afraid. Ready. Not ready.

We can plan for many elements of dying. We can write a will, decide what music we want to hear and how to dispose of our bodies. But even if I choose assistance in dying and drink the medication with my own hands, I haven't chosen to die. Death is choosing me. The illusion is that we can be in charge of the *fact* that we die.

The older I get, the easier this seems. I am beginning to accept that sometimes I need extra help, and to not see it as a reflection on my worth. I see that autonomy isn't necessarily physical. True self-determination—as refugees and prisoners show us every day—is the freedom to hold one's own ideas, to live, however confined, in a spacious mind. It is becoming easier for me to see that my body is not a reflection of my worth. It's easier, but that doesn't mean it's easy. I am a little less flexible about all this change than I would have predicted.

Statues and pictures of the death of the historical Buddha are invariably images of stillness and serenity. The traditional "dying Buddha" lies on his right side, his robes neatly arranged, eyes closed, face composed in a quiet near smile. But the prince who was surprised to discover that sickness existed died from food poisoning. He was an old man by then. He walked until he couldn't walk anymore, then sat under a tree, and then lay down in a public place. He is said to have died from the effects either of mushrooms or bad pork; in either case, that would mean vomiting, cramps, and bloody diarrhea. His followers gathered around him and he told them not to turn away. "Look," he said. "You too. This too."

This comes to you and you and you. This is part of our *nature*, this is part of *your life*, of how you live, of what it means to be human. Why would you turn away?

The statues lie about one thing, but they tell the truth about another. We may be in extremis and still at ease. The Buddha's dignity had nothing to do with the dissolution of compounded things and everything to do with understanding that compounded things always dissolve. Dignity is an expression of this greatest of freedoms: to not be disturbed by what happens to the body.

A funny story about control and how mastery of this kind stays with me. Some years ago, I was teaching a workshop on these matters of death and dying with my friend Jill, also a Zen teacher. I spoke briefly in introduction and then handed off to Jill to tell a few stories about her experience as a hospice volunteer.

After about ten minutes, she stopped talking. She just gazed down at her notes in silence. Finally she looked at me and said, "I seem to have lost my place." That was all she said. Eventually I asked the group to take a break and went over to her.

"What's up?" I asked her.

"Why am I here?" she asked, peering at me intently. "Why are *you* here?"

There was a doctor and another nurse there, and we took Jill into another room and checked her out. She knew who she was, but not where she was or her birth date or what she'd had for breakfast. Seizure? Stroke? Many possibilities. She couldn't retain any of the information we told her. For the twentieth time, she asked me why we were there. I said we were teaching a workshop on death and dying, and she said, "I must be here for show-and-tell." Over the next twenty minutes she made that joke several more times.

We sent her to the emergency room and they sent her to the ICU for the night, where she had the same circular conversations with the doctors and nurses—"Why am I here? Why are *you* here?"—and made the same joke about show-and-tell many times. Eventually she was diagnosed with an uncommon, benign condition called transient global amnesia. She simply didn't make memories for about twenty-four hours.

Jill couldn't remember anything that happened in that period, but she was still herself: blunt, curious, impatient, and witty. The qualities I think of when I think of Jill were still there, though her mind seemed to be more or less on vacation. To this day she doesn't remember going to the workshop or being sent to the hospital. The essential, conscious "I" we value so much—the self in control, making decisions—was gone. Yet the person we knew was still there. The quirks and texture of the unique Jill never left. When she made a caustic comment about show-and-tell, she became the joke in a way quite delightful to many of us with a dark Zen sense of humor. Surely, we've all been that exhibit at one time or another. I pulled the workshop back together and we went on without her. At some point, before we knew the outcome, someone brightly said, "Wouldn't it be wonderful if she died while teaching a death-and-dying workshop?" In a way, she did.

I still find Jill's odd missing day reassuring. It was a practical demonstration of what remains when the brain takes a hike. We may somehow still be present when we can't control our bodies or take care of ourselves or make decisions. Attitude leads us—attitude, and habits of mind. I want to meet death with curiosity and willingness. What do you want to do? Do you want to meet death with devotion, love, a sense of adventure, or do you want to rage against the failing light? Cultivate those qualities now. Master them. Then you will have a deep and not even conscious attitude—a mastered reaction set, as it were, that stays with you even when the mind is going. When I find myself in a new situation, when I'm scared, I try to feel curiosity even in the midst of fear. I consider the bus sliding up onto the sidewalk behind me. I consider the heart attack. The meteor. Can I be curious about the meteor? Time is a plastic thing. If I experience curiosity in the midst of fear often enough, it will be there when I need it the most.

Death will be full of surprises. Tibetan Buddhists practice dying through special meditations and visualizations, so that they will recognize the experience when it happens and not be caught off guard. They think of death as a long process, beginning before the body ceases to function and unfolding over days, weeks, even years. Tibetan Buddhism teaches that immediately after death, a person enters the so-called bardo planes, intermediate states after death and before rebirth. People who have been revived after clinical death do say they didn't realize they were dead at first. The elaborate teachings given at the moments around death are partly devoted to telling a person that he has died. "Pay attention: you are dead!" say the exhortations. Pay attention! As peaceful as the dying body can seem, would we be surprised to discover this is a time of great chaos? We are undone. Consciousness is no longer grounded in the body; perception and sensation are unraveling. The entire braid of the self is coming unwound in a rush. One's point of view must change dramatically. Being comfortable with surprise allows us to meet the unexpected, both in events and within ourselves. This curiosity will serve us well when there is nothing else to be done.

✻　　✻　　✻

When Perry was dying, a few people felt that he wasn't competent to make important decisions for himself. In much the same way that we may think a murderer is insane by virtue of the act, a few members of Perry's home care team felt that no mentally responsible person would do what Perry was doing. Why would you choose a death with, as one woman said with a grimace, such *indignity*? Why would you choose pain? We can think of a lot of pathological explanations for Perry's choice. But most would be too simple. Illness has meaning, different for each person. It may be a punishment or a challenge or the natural way of things. It may be a terrible insult. Illness and pain always have meaning— sometimes dense and subtle meaning invisible to everyone else. The life leads to the death. What did pain and the unraveling of his body mean to Perry? I don't know, but it clearly meant something important. He paid attention to it.

Compassion means to suffer with another. To be at the bedside of a dying person means to suffer dying, in a way. But it also means witnessing while a person suffers their own suffering. We have the urge to act in loco parentis to the dying. We do this in big ways ("Of *course* you're going to have surgery!") and small ("Of *course* you want to eat lunch!"). We may ignore a person's wishes, or label their wishes deviant when we don't agree. I catch myself being parental in all kinds of little ways at the bedside. I want to turn off the television because I am not going to want to watch *Judge Judy* when it's my turn and I think quiet is good for you sometimes. I don't stop to ask if the person in bed likes *Judge Judy*. I want to open the curtains because I like sunshine. It's easy to extend this to mood, food, pain, prayers. This urge can drive

you to overwhelm a person with care. Do you just have to give
that pill? Do you just have to serve that cup of tea? Are you trying,
not to relieve a person's suffering, but to take it from him? We can
smother a person's struggle with a cup of tea, and we can do it
with opinions and ideals.

My friend Carol spent a lot of time in the high desert of eastern
Oregon, where herds of antelope live. Over many summers, she
helped take down old barbed wire fences across rangeland. She
saw that the antelope would come to a place where there had been
a fence and stop. "It's as though they assume the fence is still there,"
she said. "Then suddenly they understand, and leap forward."

Carol and I talked on Christmas Eve. I had not seen her for
more than a week, because a severe snowstorm had made the
forty miles between us difficult. On our last visit, we had cleaned
out her closet. She pulled on the skinny jeans she hadn't been able
to wear since college. "Nice to be thin again," she said, "though
I wouldn't have picked this diet." She spent a lot of time in bed
by then. She loved the snow and didn't mind watching the world
turn white and clean. When I called, we didn't talk for long, because she was having trouble swallowing again. "I'm very tired,"
she said, and I could hear it in her voice. This was a new kind of
tired.

She had asked me to be her second health care representative
after her husband. I went to her chemotherapy appointments
with her and took notes when she met with her oncologist and
got bad news. But when I asked her for details about the kind of
wishes you would put on an advance directive, she wouldn't answer. "It won't be up to me," she said. She was with Epicurus, in
a way: chances were she wasn't going to be aware that decisions
were being made, so she wouldn't tell me how to decide. I had

to be satisfied with that. I did know her very well; we had talked about our lives and how we saw the world and nature many times, and I felt I knew what would be a good death for her. I could see her in the big bed in the bedroom in the house they'd built, looking out at the snow-covered fir trees that surrounded her. I could see her sliding into sleep. I knew it wouldn't be much longer; I would have to visit as soon as the snow let me up the mountain.

But. But Carol died two days later at the hospital, while a team tried to resuscitate her. She had difficulty breathing that morning, and asked her husband to get her help. David somehow got her through the snow, down the hill, to town. Her heart stopped in the emergency room and they started CPR.

A quote from my giant palliative nursing textbook: "The use of CPR negates the possibility of a peaceful death. This is considered the gravest of poor outcomes." Her death didn't look the way I thought it would, the way I thought it *should*. For a long time, I felt that her death was unfortunate, emergent, and invasive. I was angry that she had died in bright lights and noise, away from home. It hurt, too, that her death had been *away from me*. For a long time after, I felt the wound of not having been there, of her not having the death I wanted her to have—that I wanted me to have with her.

I do believe that CPR, like all kinds of supposedly life-supporting treatments, interferes with a peaceful death. But perhaps that is not true every single time. Is it possible to have a good death in the midst of desperately trying to stay alive? Once upon a time, I would have said no, not possible. And now I think: maybe, sometimes. I learned a lesson with Carol. Oh, what a hard lesson. I was selfish. I felt wounded by her death until I accepted what I already knew: Carol wanted to live, even when she was just about ready to die. It was her choice to go to the hospital. She knew she was dying and she chose to ask for help, to ask for everything. I had a fantasy about how Carol would die, a fantasy I didn't recognize as such until it was extinguished by reality. But it wasn't Carol's fantasy. What she wanted was to live and she died trying to do that, and how can I say that wasn't good? She chose it.

She always said she planned to come back as a dolphin, but I think of Carol as an antelope now: stopping where there used to be a fence, and then seeing the way clear.

All these deaths I've described can be called good deaths. The motorcyclist, who I discovered had gone to my daughter's high school, who died the day before my son's birthday in front of my house and more or less in my hands, was racing down a hill on a cool spring evening with his friend. He was riding his good bike. Afterward I read everything I could find about him. He had owned a construction business, he had loved to fish, he had really loved to ride that bike. They had climbed on their bikes, they had crested the hill, and in a second he was dead. Was this a bad death? I doubt he had seen it coming. He was here and then he was not, all at once.

By most definitions of a good death, Perry didn't have one. He was in pain and surely had unrelieved sorrow. Those who witnessed it—those who formed both the professional and the social components of his death—were in distress. He had almost no autonomy. But I think that what Perry was trying to tell us by refusing our well-intentioned care was that he had no other power. No power in the most fundamental sense; his was the molecular powerlessness of the body. He understood that death was making the decisions. The one choice that mattered most to him was the one he didn't have: he had to die.

All the planning and support and advance directives in the world won't give you *control*. These are the things we cannot control: we are animals, our bodies fail, and we cannot stop dying. Perry saw a force much greater than himself. So I call his a death claimed, a death unhidden. A good death.

4

Communication

A few months before Carol died, when she could no longer walk more than a few steps, she asked me to help her choose what she would be buried in. I found a small store that sold biodegradable coffins and shrouds. I went shopping, talked with the clerk, compared prices and decomposition times and delivery schedules. I brought back pamphlets. We talked about a muslin shroud versus hemp. Or maybe the willow coffin. Maybe the cardboard, because her friends could write on that one. Carol settled on a muslin shroud and a cardboard bier. They arrived a short while later in neat packages.

I write that so calmly. I wasn't calm. I hated that conversation. Carol was in a wheelchair in her living room, in the log home she and her husband had built by hand, beside the piano I sometimes played. The house was familiar to me, its smells, the sound of the dogs' toenails on the floor, the creak of the staircase. We sat together and looked at the tall pines and the autumn sky. She, who had been invincible, was pale and cold. "I want the shroud," she said. We talked quietly. No drama. Just one conversation among thousands. But I knew better and I think Carol knew better. Larry Hjort, an AIDS activist, gave counsel to people who were overwhelmed with the needs of their dying friends. "Everyone is perfectly adequate," he said. "There are just some impossible situations." How can we accept that we will die? It's impossible! How do we prepare to lose those we love? The entire experience is ridiculous, hard to comprehend at times.

She had not wanted to talk about any details since she'd finished chemotherapy. After all we'd done and said together in decades of friendship, we shied away from the pain of details at times. That day, we were talking about the world. About everything. We had different vocabularies, but we knew each other's language fairly well. Such moments can take your breath away, moments when all excess and decoration is removed. I was in an altered state for hours. And Carol, of course, was in an altered state all the time. She was dying.

If you are dying, you can say anything you want. You can say it when you want, and to whom you want. And you don't have to say anything at all. Most of what I offer here is for the visitor, the companion, the helper. You have to follow some rules.

Think about how you explain ordinary information: the washing machine is on the fritz, we're out of milk, I got a parking ticket today. Then think about how you communicate more urgent news: I wrecked the car. The power's out. It's different. Consider how you react in an argument. That's different, too. Do you shut down, stop thinking? Do you start to cry or yell or leave the room? We all have a pattern for difficult conversations. If you are going to spend time with a dying person, know how you handle emotional scenes. What scares you? What makes it easier? Make a list. Practice!

Listening isn't that complicated. It's hard, but it's not complicated. Few of us communicate really well. We think explaining ourselves is key, but listening is the most important part. Half the energy of caring for a dying person is listening, *really* listening. We are driven to think of ourselves first, and spend half the time appearing to listen while we prepare what we are going to say when it is our turn to speak. So: Listen. Say: *This sounds very difficult.* Say: *I can tell how much thinking you've done about this matter.* Say: *Um-hmm. Tell me more.* Keep bringing your mind back to the present moment when you stray. Invite detail. Ask questions and make it clear that you want to know. Anxiety makes it difficult to remember information, so repeat yourself if necessary. Speak in a calm and unhurried way. Reflect what you've heard, because you might have heard wrong: *It sounds like you are saying you are afraid.* Clarify, because you might have heard wrong: *Let me make sure I understand. I think you are saying—* If you can do these things, you are almost there. Be calm. Be nonjudgmental. Repeat.

If you are spending time with a person who is dying, you become a protector. You are the defender of modesty, privacy, silence, laughter, and many other things that can be lost in the daily tasks. You are the guardian of that person's desires.

You will become a gatekeeper. Everyone needs a gatekeeper! Be the one who can say with a smile, *Goodbye, Aunt Lucille.* The one who can reach out a hand to the visitor and say, *Time to go. We'll call when we're ready for another visit!* while walking to the door.

Visitors come in many forms. Lots of friends will just drop in for a cup of tea and a few innings of the baseball game and take the garbage out when they go. Hurray for those friends. But you may also meet what the writer Glennon Doyle calls the Fixer. This is the person who "is certain that my situation is a question and she knows the answer." The Fixer is on the edge of her seat, ready with the solution. Doyle went through a difficult breakup, and so she also knows the Comparer: the visitor who only appears to listen, who is just waiting for the chance to explain how his experience, or his nephew's experience, or his aunt's boyfriend's cousin's experience, compares to yours. Sooner or later a visitor arrives with what I think of as one-downs-manship: the person with the sad face who spends their entire visit explaining why their troubles are worse than yours.

Set boundaries—for visitors, but also for yourself. Start with setting the boundaries for the visit, and do this every time. Say, *I can stay for an hour*, or *I'll be here until dinner, when Mary arrives*. Before you leave, tell the person when you will be back. This removes the uncertainty, the unbounded edges that can make for a stressful conversation. A boundary gives both of you a space in which to be together. If you're going to be coming regularly, you might offer a frank contract: when you will be there, for how long, to do what. If you can't stand daytime television, can you watch *Days of Our Lives* anyway? If you don't like cigarettes, can you sit easily with someone who smokes? Don't say: *I told you to quit smoking*.

There are lots of ways to help besides making soup and sweeping the floor. (Those are often good things to do.) You can help people write letters or arrange a meeting. Offer to buy groceries or do the laundry, drive to an appointment or organize the bills. Offer only what you can deliver: *I will stay with you through the night*, or *I will mail these letters for you*. Be specific. (Then *do* what you say you will do. Not to put too fine a point on it, but you only get one shot at this.) Write all these things down and put it on the refrigerator. Your friend has enough to remember without keeping track of the calendar. Don't say: *Be sure to keep me posted.*

Ask permission for everything. Be aware that you have the power here. (Be willing to discuss this fact.) Ask permission until your friend says, *Quit asking for permission.* Ask if a person wants to talk before you plunge in with news of the day. Would they rather listen to music or play checkers or watch *The Walking Dead*? Do they want to take a shower? Do they want to eat something? If so, be clear. *Vanilla or chocolate ice cream?* is easier to answer than *Is there anything you want to eat?* Always ask for permission, but give permission, too. Permission to be sad, to be angry, to be sleepy or bored. To be something other than dying. To die.

Ask about privacy and confidentiality, favorite foods, how they want the room to be set up. Lights up, or down? Door open or closed? Music on or off? Agree on a signal for ending the visit. Know when to leave. Know when to be quiet.

You have to be honest with the dying person, but above all with yourself. There is nothing else worth doing here. Honesty is generosity, because when you are honest, you offer what you can truly give. Be honest about your own emotional state, without burdening the sick person. Defend against your own impulses, your need for consolation, your wish for power, your urge for denial.

Know your limits. You have to grieve, and that means you have to go away sometimes. If you are hungry or need a rest, take care of yourself. If you're anxious or worried, admit it. (Just don't ask your friend to fix your feeling.) There's a tricky balance between keeping your feelings in check and being authentic. You may try to downplay things, especially tears and anger, but you don't have to hide them completely. On the other hand, you may be surprised by jealousy, irritation, and loneliness, and these are really yours to sort out elsewhere. Don't say: *Why didn't you call me first? Why did you tell her before me?*

Knowing these things is half the battle. The other half is watching and working with what happens.

A person who is ill may try to trigger your reactions. People may be testing whether you can handle talking about a difficult subject. Good listening goes a long way toward showing acceptance, and so does an open posture. Don't stand over a person in bed or bustle around when they're talking. Settle down, relax, keep your posture open, and try not to touch or brush away the difficulties. You might feel a powerful urge to soothe painful feelings, to cover up. Don't change the subject.

If there is a topic you absolutely cannot discuss, make that clear. Can you be still while a person cries? Don't put a person in the difficult position of upsetting his caregiver. Don't hide all your feelings under a bushel, but be a grown-up and manage your grown-up pain.

A person overwhelmed with illness may displace difficult feelings and shift attention away from the problem she is afraid to face. The big problem at hand. The ego is often about seven years old and prone to distractions when uncomfortable, like a kid who spills his milk just as you ask whether his chores are done. Adaptation takes many forms. Some people rationalize destructive behavior, ignore consequences. Some people will regress under stress, reverting to behaviors they used when they were much younger, refusing to take responsibility and looking for another person to act as the adult. There's nothing inherently wrong with that; we all like someone else to be the adult sometimes. Just notice if it's a pattern, and be careful. Watch the urge to become parental under stress, to take charge and try to manage the situation. Taking charge protects you from having to feel helpless, but may not be what the person really needs.

Balance affect. If the person is hurried and talkative, you can speak slowly and listen. If they are withdrawn, you can start by doing the talking. If they are pacing, sit still. Notice incongruence. Is the person smiling while they tell a sad story? Are they clenching their fists when they say everything is fine? Dying tends to create incongruent feelings. You don't have to challenge this. The person is working things out. Just be congruent in yourself. Don't be afraid to cry a little sometimes; that's congruent.

One way I might manage the hardest parts of being sick is to intellectualize my feelings. Perhaps I talk about the kind and brand of walker I want and ask you to check on prices. But I never say how it feels to need a walker (or a burial shroud). I may complain about how long it takes you to bring me lunch because I don't want you to notice that I need help getting up from my chair. I don't want to notice it, either. If I get angry at you for being late, I can briefly forget how it feels to need your help in the first place. Humans deflect when things hurt, and we are quick to project our struggles onto other people, using another as a kind of surrogate. I may talk about how Uncle Mario needs to use a walker now. I'm not just distracting you; I'm also testing you. I'm learning important information on how you feel about people who need walkers.

What not to say: *Don't talk like that. Let's just talk about something happy.* One of the most common ways we defend ourselves is by denial. We may simply deny that what we've been told is true. Things not to say: *My mother's biopsy was negative. You look fine. Are you sure you're sick?* Denial is normal, but notice your own. A dying person may deny the truth for a long time. How often do we deny another's denial? How often do we try to drag a person to the place we think they *should* be, instead of meeting a person where he or she is? This is where open-ended responses help so much. Reflect what you hear. Ask for more detail. Ask what it means. Listen.

My friend Marc had Hodgkin's disease for many years. He had long remissions and several relapses, years of feeling better, then worse. Finally he entered an experimental drug program at Sloan Kettering. After a few months he suddenly became quite ill, his body shutting down all at once, and he was admitted to the ICU.

Marc was a fellow Buddhist teacher and a lawyer. He taught meditation at Seton Hall, where he was on faculty. We had talked many times about his health—frank conversations in which he mused about having limited time, about not knowing if he would live a few more years or a few more months. With that in mind, we talked about treatment options and whether he should keep driving during chemotherapy and whether he'd be able to keep off the weight he'd lost and how it felt to go on dates now.

I spoke to him two days before he died. He was on the other side of the country from me and I knew I would never see him again. He was on a ventilator, but conscious. I am told he smiled and nodded his head when I told him I was thinking about him and wishing him well, and that he gave me a thumbs-up when I told him a lame Zen joke. The next day his sister called me. She was in distress; Marc had lost consciousness and they didn't know what to do. It was only then that I realized he had no plans for his actual death. He had written nothing down, given no instructions, even after being admitted to the ICU, even after needing to be put on a ventilator. In all our conversations, we had never discussed his actual death. He knew he was *going* to die but hadn't told me *how* he wanted to die. Nor had he told his doctors, his religious teacher, his beloved sister, or any of his many friends. I hadn't asked him about it because he lived thousands of miles away and we saw each other only once or twice a year. I just *assumed*. I assumed he would have told me if he'd wanted me to be involved. I assumed he did tell others. We all assumed, I think, that someone else knew.

Don't say: *Stop, you're making me sad. Don't be so negative.* But if a dying person says this, you'd better change the subject. Denial can be exactly what a family wants; families can cultivate denial and resist the truth. Don't say: *Our neighbor's daughter had this and she's fine now.* We indulge in denial and we fight the denial of others. Why isn't Uncle Phil *realistic*? One way to cope is to get busy, plunging into the truth. We want to get palliative care started. We want to help our loved one avoid unnecessary procedures and save money. We want plans to get made so our own suffering can finally end. But part of loving a person may be allowing denial to exist as long as it exists. In a few cases, that's until death.

Don't say: *Face the music. My mother had this and she was dead in three months.* You may feel such a need to comfort the person that you cover up the truth. Or you may feel—as I often did with my mother—such a need to talk about the elephant in the room that you undermine their shaky sense of safety. Your unfinished business is no one's problem but your own.

People who are dying will try out a number of ways to respond to the impossible fact. A person may say something that sounds completely hopeless. *There's no point. It's no good. This won't work.* He may be trying out this possibility. (At some point, this will be true.) A person may say things that sound ridiculously optimistic. *I'll be skiing in Aspen by Christmas.* She may just want to feel better for a time. Hope can be comforting, and hope can cause a lot of pain. Sometimes those close to a dying person can disrupt the natural process of grief by playing on—or against—hope. It's not very helpful to say, *You're going to be fine!* People know when they are dying. They don't need to be protected from the knowledge, though doing so is common in many cultures. Above all, if you are talking with a person who is dying, be aware of what *you* want and what you think the dying person *should* do and *should* feel, and keep it to yourself.

Your friend knows why you are there. Nigel Barley writes, "If the road to Hell is paved with good intentions, the road to death is paved with platitudes." Don't use euphemisms unless you are asked to do so by the dying person. (Even *end-of-life care* is a kind of euphemism, a way of focusing attention on the life instead of the death. We are at the end of a life, and the care we are giving and receiving is care unique to the last of one's life. But be careful not to use that phrase as a way to avoid saying *death*.)

Don't make promises. Don't tell lies. Every time you lie, or just pretend things are different, you lose trust. Doctors and families and patients all lie, knowing better. As Cory Taylor wrote when she was dying from melanoma, "In hospitals we don't talk about death; we talk about treatment." Doctors have all kinds of imperfect human reasons to lie about a prognosis, try to override your wishes, or obfuscate when questioned. It's hard to lose a patient you've come to like; it's hard to fail at a cure; it's hard to think, however erroneously, that there is nothing more to offer. Treatment means control. It means success. As the gatekeeper, you may at times be a witness for medical truth, taking notes at an exam, keeping a list of questions, and blocking the door until your friend gets answers. Don't say: *Be nice to the doctor.* Do say: *Doctor, can you explain that in lay terms, please?*

Don't offer advice unless you are clearly asked for it. And if you are asked for advice, give it gently and openly, leaving room for differences. Don't try to cheer a person up. Please don't say: *Practice gratitude.* And don't "Kübler-Ross" a person. Don't say: *I see you're in the bargaining stage.* Don't assume you understand a person's reasons for their behavior.

Don't make this kind of comment: *I'll pray for you.* Don't say: *This is a blessing in disguise. This is an opportunity.* These words separate us, driving a wedge of belief and faith and intention and commitment between us. Unless you know the dying person very well, and are sure—I mean really sure—that the person shares your worldview, don't even offer. Don't ever say: *I'm sure God has a plan.*

Don't say: *If I were you . . .* Your friend wishes it *was* you. You can help with practical details and planning. But—oh, this is such a big but—only when and if the person agrees to the help. Offer, then *shut up.* A person will get ready when he or she is ready to get ready. When I think about Marc, I wonder if he just wasn't, not even at the end, not even then. Not even then. Perhaps he was trying to protect his family and his friends—and perhaps himself. He was focused on treatment; the decline came very fast and took a lot of people by surprise. But if I could do it again, at least I would ask. I would ask once. Maybe twice. Then I would shut up.

Notice if you're inserting yourself into the situation. Notice if your mouth starts to form the words *I think you should* or *Why don't you . . .* (Silence first. Notice the reaction, notice the words forming, the urge to rescue, fix, deny, demand, direct, avoid, confront. Notice the words and let them go, and start again.) Beware of your own bias. (Things not to say: *You should quit eating sugar. Have you tried meditation? You should read this great book about mindfulness and cancer.*)

Dying is very intimate, but don't take things too personally. Respect privacy. Don't presume you have the right to know everything, to see anything, to have a single one of your questions answered. Glennon Doyle calls a certain kind of visitor the Reporter, the one who "asks inappropriate, probing questions and her eyes glisten as she waits for the answers." The Reporter, of course, needs to report; she immediately shares your details with others, stealing a little of the tragedy for her own. (What not to say: *Tell me* all *about it.*) When people are sick, and already losing autonomy, and taking off their clothes for doctors and nurses, and getting stuck and cathed and scanned, they may feel more reserved than usual when they have the chance. When people see that their modesty will be overwhelmed by their illness—annihilated by it until every inch is exposed—they may not want to tell you the latest lab results. Or let you help them to the bathroom. Or answer one single question more. Talk about something else.

Don't predict how long a person will live. Don't say: *Are you sure that doctor knows what he's talking about?* Don't say: *Why don't you try harder? Don't you love me enough to fight?* Don't say: *You meant so much to me*—forgetting to change the tense. Don't say, never say, do not say: *Help me get through this.* Never complain that a person's death is difficult for you to bear. (I've read more than one story about a visitor who actually said, "This is harder on me than it is on you.") The dying person has no obligation to sort things out for you, listen to your apologies, explain his past actions, or make you feel better about his death. It is not the dying person's job to fix your loss of him. This sounds so obvious, but the urge to be consoled in our grief is great. *Don't leave me,* you think. *How can you? What will I do? Why is this happening? Fix it.* These thoughts make no logical sense, yet you may feel a powerful need to say them out loud. Don't. A dying person truly needs to know that their death will not cause harm. It hurts—of course it hurts—but no one is trying to hurt you.

Accept what a person says. Period. Accept what the person says about her emotional state, her thoughts about heaven, his fears about pain, his certainty of a cure. Like everyone else, a dying person may be irritable, dark of wit, depressed, or withdrawn. Trying to cheer a person up is disrespectful and shows a lack of attention. The person may start a serious conversation and then change the subject. They may repeat themselves many times. They may refuse to say goodbye. The dying person may be happy one moment and crying the next, more interested in how the Mets are doing than his wound care, and appear more worried about the fate of a television character than their own. A dying person may book a vacation you know they will never take, plant a tree, buy a car, and shave their head. Make room for rage. Make room for clarity and insight, composure and acceptance, and throwing the bedpan across the room. Make room for the possibility of changing the course of a life, even at the last moment. Make room for a person to transform, to express love, perhaps for the first time.

They are working it out. You should be, too.

5

Last Months

Grandpa's funeral was just the tip of the iceberg in my family. My heritage is Scottish, Irish, and English. My family came to the United States many generations ago on what are sometimes called "coffin ships" for their dismal conditions, and became farmers, homesteaders, and Oregon Trail pioneers: not exactly stoic, but tough stock not given to display. My maternal grandfather died more or less without acknowledgment, and about a decade later my grandmother died, and again the details were not up for discussion.

When my mother was diagnosed with breast cancer, she begged me not to ask the doctor questions; she "didn't want to bother him." She died less than two years later, and we never talked explicitly about her illness. Near the end of her life, she was sleeping in a hospital bed in the living room. One day when I was visiting, she asked me to get her jewelry box—the same big jewelry box she had had all my life, filled with the same costume jewelry she had always worn. For a few hours she carefully divided everything in the box between my sister and me. She did not say why. Not then, not ever, did she acknowledge in words that she was going to die. But from that day on, she started sorting.

There are as many ways to be as there are people on this earth. We are conditioned creatures, made out of habit and influence that begins before we are born. A serious illness exquisitely frames one's background. I don't mean to be academic here; this feels real and personal to me, that I am made of so many things given to me by others—by genetics, history, relationship, experience.

Ethnicity is often the strongest influence on us, and illness brings this into strong focus: ethnic backgrounds support us with tradition and shared values when we most need a foundation. Like me, you probably find such support to be both consoling and constricting. While it derives from one's race and place of origin, ethnicity is really about relationships: how the whole matrix of family works together, all those group behaviors and expectations you learned as a child, enjoyed over vacations when you came back for visits, and perhaps left behind with a small sigh of relief. A member from one group immediately calls for help in a crisis and the family converges on the sick member for weeks, brooking no dissent, filling the room. A member from another group—say, working-class Anglo-Saxon Protestant pioneers—may never talk about the illness, ask for a prognosis, or admit she is dying. The family stands by, assenting to the silence, waiting for her to sort the earrings. I've worked hard to overcome it, but the hardworking, buttoned-up people who are my ancestors and relatives left a mark on me. I'm much more willing to divulge private matters and share complaints than my mother and I bug my doctor every which way. But I have a deep and surprising instinct for privacy, too. Serious illness confuses the issue; early conditioning meets an adult who has traveled a long way away.

Chronic illness is a big challenge to one person and just another chapter to another. Everything comes into play: mental and physical strength, education and income, gender and sexuality, age, occupation, religion. Our net worth drives our access to health care in the first place; people with higher incomes simply live longer because of this, and have far more choices when they are ill or dying. People who are not used to good health care may not even know what kind of help is possible, or how to ask for it, and be submissive to medical authority out of the belief they have no choice. The fear of a financial disaster for one's family is real (and so are the disasters). Illness means bills, and it means lost work, and eventually a lost identity. Older people may also be more submissive, but this could change as my entitled generation ages a bit more.

I worked on an inpatient oncology unit before marriage equality. We would ask the same-gender partner of a patient, "You *are* the legal representative, right?" and not really wait for an answer, because we wanted the patient's partner to feel welcome even if the laws said otherwise. People with fluid gender or sexual orientation learn early on to be skeptical of the health care system, and sidle up to it with trepidation. Immigrants may do this, too, and non-native English speakers, as well as people of certain religions who, like people in the LGBTQ community, have learned to expect misunderstanding.

I have had a few serious illnesses and several surgeries, but I never really felt like a *sick person*. I consider myself healthy, even vigorous—unrealistically so, sometimes. I was a healthy child, a strong child, and this burrowed into me, into who I thought myself to be. And so I'm not a very good patient when illness interrupts: I get annoyed, I feel sorry for myself, I complain and resist treatment. Eventually all of us will be overtaken by frailty, and frailty, in whatever form, becomes the focus, and other selves fall away.

When Paul Kalanathi was in treatment for cancer, he found that he had to let go of roles he wasn't even aware of inhabiting— not just the obvious roles, like doctor, but more subtle ones, like that of the strong, active man, the leader, the decision maker. The role of being a good-looking man: "Any part of me that identified with being handsome was slowly being erased."

We can resist this. I may be a person with cancer, a person who can no longer work or live alone or button her own shirt. I may even be a terminally ill person. But I am also a person who reads books and likes ice cream. Sick people need to not be sick people all the time. They are also plumbers, parents, students, friends, chess players. A person who has been healthy may cling to the details of these roles for a long time. (A person who has embraced the sick role may try to avoid them altogether.) Don't forget who this person in front of you is, his complexity, her history.

Dying includes times of being very vulnerable and broken. The old self is gone. The new self is being discovered. Grief begins with diagnosis: *Why me? Why not me?* Coming to terms with terminal illness requires a time of darkness, a natural introspection. How this looks and how long it lasts will be different for each of us. The first and one of the hardest tasks of dying and caring for the dying is to accept that things will never be the same. *Things will never be the same.* The body will never be the same. Relationships will never be the same. *Nothing* will be the same as it was.

Yet there is liberation—an unexpected, gentle release from all kinds of rules. As the writer Marjorie Gross noted after she was diagnosed with ovarian cancer, "Suddenly, everything has a life-time guarantee." She doesn't want to paint "too bleak a picture," Gross writes, since terminal cancer has a number of benefits: "People don't ask you to help them move" and "You never have to wait in line for anything again. Take off the hat and get whisked to the front."

June Bingham, a playwright and author, was diagnosed with metastatic cancer at the age of eighty-eight and decided not to have treatment. She turned toward her death with wit and ease, freed, she wrote, from competition and the need to look in mirrors. She canceled the tedious visits to the dentist, eye doctor, and dermatologist that had filled too many of her days. She and her husband stopped buying theater tickets and planning day trips and, as she wrote in an essay with apparent satisfaction, ordering new stationery. They "have thrown caution to the winds and now buy 2-percent milk instead of the boring 1-percent," she added. "We also make club sandwiches with white bread."

This is not to say that we don't lie to ourselves. Do I believe that my meditation practice will somehow allow me to slide past the suffering? A little bit. Do I think I can avoid the anxiety or sorrow of the diagnosis, be always in equanimity, a model to others? You bet. Loss and grief are universal; sometimes I think hubris almost is. There is no way to vaccinate ourselves. *All that is dear to me and everyone I love are of the nature to change. There is no way to escape being separated from them.* Impossible! We don't get to skip stages or avoid pain. If I am truly honest with myself, all I have learned is to see how much I want to avoid not only pain but being seen to want to avoid it.

Bargaining, which comes and goes, may be done in secret. A private prayer, a secret vow, a promise only the dying person knows. Dying people don't lose hope; it just changes. First, you hope for a mistake. *What a quack that doctor is. How could the lab mix things up that way?* Next, you hope for a cure. A new treatment. A miracle! Hope is a lot like fear; both are based on what might happen. Hoping for a cure and fearing there isn't one are versions of the same thought: *I'm not going to die.* Honest hope is hope for good days, for a chance to finish a project, see a person one more time, get to the nephew's graduation, repair a broken friendship. Write a song. Clean a closet. Hope never goes away. Adults in both the United States and New Zealand, where the seasons are reversed, are still more likely to die of natural causes between Christmas and New Year's than at any other time of the year. Holidays matter. In time, a person who is terminally ill will start hoping simply for time, and comforts: to walk a few steps, eat, take Communion, have one more bowl of ice cream.

The changes we experience with dying from a long illness depend on the cause, but certain ones are common to almost everyone. Fatigue is our companion. Fatigue is not tiredness or lack of sleep. It is not depression. Fatigue in advanced disease is mysterious; one textbook lists nine different theories to explain it. For one, it may be partly anemia; for another, an accumulation of toxins, and for another, fatigue follows treatment; cancer chemotherapy is notorious for this. But fatigue is more than these obvious physical changes. True fatigue seems to steal the vital, core energy. One literally lacks. Fatigue is persistent, intense, distressing—a lack of energy so complete, people may have trouble opening their eyes, lifting a hand, speaking. If you are tired, you may not want to climb the stairs, but you will if the baby is crying or the fire alarm goes off. If you are fatigued, you may not able to climb the stairs no matter what.

Mild, regular exercise helps. This doesn't necessarily mean the treadmill. It might mean going to work one or two days a week, a slow walk around the block, or simply sitting up for a meal. Exercise is whatever puts a little stress on the body, stretches you just a little. Mainly, you adjust. You are left out of things. You begin to see the way you identify yourself with what you are able to do. (What not to say: *I'm going to Bermuda this summer. What are* you *doing for vacation?*)

Fatigue changes things, but it doesn't stop everything. Carol went on a safari to South Africa the year before she died, in the midst of chemotherapy. She had wanted to go on that trip for many years, had saved money and planned it in great detail, and even when she spiked a fever just before they left, she went. The trip wasn't what she'd imagined: she had to calculate everything from the number of miles she could travel in a day to the kind of food she was able to eat. But she went on that damned safari. Seven months before she died, we went to Belize. We traveled much more slowly than we used to, took more days off. She slept a lot. But we rode the bus down the Hummingbird Highway and took the fast little boat out to the islands. We dove—not as frequently as before, or as deep or for as long, but we were in the water every day. On Carol's last scuba dive, we didn't go far. The water was transparent and warm, a pale blue and gold. We held hands, because she felt safer that way, and just looked at this world we had come to know and explored together. We both knew it was the last time. I helped her to climb up the ladder that she used to scramble up without a thought. But there we were, on our beloved blue water, sticky and wet and tired, very tired, and glad.

Pain. The most common fear, but often the fear is not realistic. Aging and terminal illness are not necessarily painful. I see many people in their eighties and nineties who are comfortable on a dose or two of acetaminophen every day. People who are dying often say they have no pain. A lot of the recent writing in the so-called death awareness movement tells terrible stories of people screaming in pain, abandoned to their suffering. I believe this happens, but I want you to believe that it doesn't have to happen. Research in hospice and palliative care shows that only about one in a hundred people has uncontrolled pain while dying. That doesn't mean no one has pain. It means that ninety-nine out of a hundred people who do have pain get relief. It is so manageable that a patient can sue a doctor if they have uncontrolled pain. If you hear such stories—*He was screaming in pain!*—you are almost always hearing a story about medical and nursing neglect.

For many people, pain is annoying. An irritation. For others, simply being too cold feels like a wound, and pain is hard to bear. For one person, pain means *I'm in trouble*; for another, pain means *I'm still alive.* What does the pain mean *to the person who has it?* People with chronic pain, such as from rheumatoid arthritis, are at risk for undertreatment of pain. They may not show signs; they have adapted, and may not grimace or moan even when the pain is difficult. Watch for more subtle signs, like muscle tension. Men are also at risk for being undertreated, reluctant to admit to having pain, because it seems like a sign of weakness. (I have found that men are more willing to take pain medication when I point out that their blood pressure has gone up.)

Pain is subjective. Pain is what a person says it is. Do not judge; you can't know. A person may appear quite comfortable and relaxed and say they have pain. They may look wretched and deny pain. You have to trust the person. People who are dying are not drug seekers: they aren't looking to get high; they aren't malingering. I know there are a lot of people who believe that there is some kind of moral lesson in having pain or that treating pain is a sign of inner weakness or that you must stay awake in order to die well or that *God will never give you more than you can handle*. Rubbish. Treat the pain until the pain is controlled, and if your doctor refuses to work with you until your pain is controlled, get a new doctor.

Pain doesn't always require strong drugs. Regular doses of acetaminophen are useful and safe in the recommended dose for most people. Cannabis is a great pain medication for many people. Meditation, visualization, and regular mild exercise can all help with pain. But there's no reason to fear narcotics if they're needed.

In medical terms, morphine is the gold standard for pain control. That means all other narcotic drugs are measured against it. In the early nineteenth century, what we now call morphine was isolated from opium, which is found in the juice of poppy seedpods—as natural as a medicine can be, if that is important to you. Since then, morphine has been used as an analgesic for severe pain—used and sometimes misused. The Brompton cocktail, a combination of morphine and cocaine, was created in the nineteenth century to treat advanced cancer. Then these two drugs were combined with alcohol, sugar, and chloroform water. In the 1950s, Cicely Saunders, leader of the nascent hospice movement in England, recommended a similar mixture, but included a tincture of cannabis. Morphine, cocaine, alcohol, sugar, chloroform, and cannabis in one nice mix; I have to assume this helped in some way. Various Brompton-type formulas became common in the United Kingdom in the 1960s and 1970s and then in the United States. But, over time, research on various combinations showed that you could take out each piece except the morphine and get the same pain relief. It was the morphine that counted.

Today, morphine in various forms is one of the most common drugs given to terminally ill people, particularly useful for pain from cancer, bone diseases, and organ failure. Morphine is cheap, comes in both short-acting and long-acting types, and is well understood—very safe when given properly.

The most common side effect of opiate drugs is sedation. This often goes away with a few days of regular use, but opiates of all kinds raise the question of balance. Do you prefer being sleepy and pain-free? Or can you tolerate moderate pain in order to be alert all day? This is the kind of information that should go in your advance directive. Morphine also causes mood changes, generally a sense of well-being or euphoria, but some people feel depressed. A few people have itching or nausea. Constipation is common.

I'm afraid of becoming addicted. Worrying about addiction is a kind of magical thinking, projecting into a future that is not really up for consideration. But, more to the point, it's very unlikely. Addiction is marked by harmful, compulsive behavior, an overwhelming need to feel the effect of the drug. Addiction is a social as well as a physical disease. If people begin to use the drug for the emotional effect, addiction can happen. If you use pain medications as they are intended—to control pain—you're not an addict.

Changes in the body do happen. When we use any of a number of drugs over time, the body will develop *tolerance*. Tolerance means that the liver is producing enzymes to metabolize the drug;

over time, higher doses will be needed for the same effect. With opiates, there are also changes in brain biochemistry that reduce a drug's effectiveness over time. Tolerance is not addiction, and it happens with nonnarcotic drugs as well. In the last few weeks or days of life, a person may take doses of morphine almost hourly to help with pain and with breathing. There is no true upper limit to the dose. In time, the body will also develop *dependence*. Dependence means that if the drug is abruptly taken away, there will be symptoms of withdrawal. Dependence by itself is not addiction, and happens with many drugs. Dependence is readily managed by reducing the amount of drug being used over time. A dying person usually has no reason to be concerned about it.

The body has a variety of opioid receptors scattered throughout the central nervous system, so morphine has other uses besides pain control. At low doses, it can suppress a chronic cough. In a way not entirely understood, morphine makes it easier for people struggling with shortness of breath to breathe more easily. Morphine slows the movements of the entire digestive system; a tincture of opium is sometimes used for severe diarrhea. For that reason, constipation is the bane of all opiates, the one side effect that never gets better. Morphine should always be prescribed with bowel medications.

And on that note: Did you flinch when you read the word *bowel*? Adults go to the bathroom alone. Adults don't soil themselves. When an adult is unable to do these things, she may feel terrible anger and shame. But sooner or later, for every single person who dies, the dying will take this control away. A person may have constipation or diarrhea or both, from the illness and from medications. He may be physically unable to control himself or even recognize the physical signals anymore. If you are going to help someone who is dying, you should be prepared to help in the toilet. Know if you have a problem with this, and be honest. If you can't be calm and cheerful in the bathroom, don't help. Don't ever say: *Time to change your diaper!*

Here's something else not to say: *You're so lucky to have lost weight.* Weight loss is normal toward the end of life. Loss of appetite—technically called anorexia—is almost universal, and certain diseases cause wasting.

A dying person may be nauseated. You can have nausea and not vomit; you can vomit without feeling nauseated; but often they go together. Most of the time, if a person has persistent nausea or vomiting, there is more than one cause: disease, like cancer; medications, like antibiotics; constipation; congestive heart failure; fluid and electrolyte imbalances; anxiety—and many other things. Nausea is very easily triggered. When I gave chemotherapy, I found that people would vomit at the smell of the alcohol pad. Be very careful about odors. Don't assume that what was pleasant last week is pleasant today. Smell is the most evocative of senses; the volatile molecules of the world enter us, literally, triggering memory and emotion, desire and disgust. Take this change seriously; it hurts to lose the pleasures of smell. Ask in advance about bringing food or flowers or using bath salts, don't wear perfume, and be careful about anything that has a strong smell. You don't want to be the most nauseating thing that happens in the day.

Nausea is subjective, like pain; believe what you are told. Because it often has more than one cause, it may be best dealt with by more than one medication. Lorazepam, an antianxiety drug, can help with nausea. Steroids are sometimes used. Remember that morphine can cause nausea. If one drug doesn't work, try another, or a combination. Don't give up. You may need to use a suppository or even an IV to get control of severe nausea. If you are vomiting, you can't keep the pills to stop the vomiting in your stomach.

Meanwhile, try this: marijuana. Pot is the most effective drug for many people, and you won't know if it works for you until you try it. Some people think its sedating qualities aren't worth the anti-nausea effect, but others aren't bothered by that. Try a cool, damp cloth on the forehead. Lying flat after a meal. Sitting up after a meal. Fresh air. Bland foods. Meditation. Acupuncture. Distraction—and I'm serious about that. Distraction really works. Take a slow walk, talk about a novel, play a video game. Experiment. Keep trying. Nausea can be a difficult symptom to manage, but not impossible.

We eat together. As universal as any human behavior is the common meal. Nausea, loss of appetite, and the resultant weight loss are distressing, since they are unavoidable signs of change. Sometimes family members are more bothered by the loss of appetite than anything else. We feed each other and share meals as an expression of love; during serious illness, making a meal can seem like the only way to help when nothing else can be done. It can be difficult to translate this intimacy into other ways of being together. I've seen family members bullying and belittling a sick person, even going into a panic as they realize what not eating implies.

This change can't be easily ignored. You have to face it. If you are helping with meals for a sick person, the most important thing to remember is that the sick person gets to decide what and how much she eats. Don't say: *If you really wanted to get well, you'd eat.* You can help a lot by making meals with small portions, setting a nice table, and then *eating with the person.* No one really wants to eat when they are surrounded by worried people who are urging them to eat. Eating together slows down your conversation, helps everyone relax, and builds trust. Share the meal.

Dying is a state of ongoing loss. Hair, teeth, erections. The ability to tie shoes or carry groceries. Breasts. Vision. Attention span. The evening walk. Driving. The strength to climb stairs, to do the laundry and housework. Bladder control, a sense of smell, balance. Relationships disappear, plans are revoked, social roles are extinguished.

One study found that 77 percent of terminally ill people were depressed. Another study found that only 15 percent of terminally ill people were depressed. Other studies fall everywhere in between these numbers. Are dying people depressed? How is *depression* defined and measured? How are those measurements interpreted? A person says, *I'm ready to die.* One witness pulls up a chair with interest; here is a sign of acceptance. Another witness sounds the alarm: Quick, suicide watch! Depression can be a rational response to a difficult situation. All of us will have periods of depression after a loss, like a breakup or unemployment. Most of us come out of that depression as time passes and the situation changes. Depression can be caused by medications or organic changes in the brain. Many signs of a clinical depression—withdrawal from social relationships, losing interest in typical activities, talking less, eating less, sleeping more, and so on—look a lot like the late stages of dying.

The experience we call *demoralization* can arise out of a sense of meaninglessness, a loss of purpose, or deep spiritual distress. A person can be demoralized without being depressed. This moment may be tolerable or even happy. But illness and physical decline is such a loss that the person sees no meaningful future ahead. A young person with ALS might be in this state; alive now, happy to be alive now, but starkly aware of the future to come. This isn't depression; it's a kind of bleak, honest appraisal of reality. ALS is one of the most common reasons for choosing not to wait for the future to arrive.

I sometimes see a sixty-two-year-old man with rapidly progressive Parkinson's disease. He is in the last months of his life now. He has trouble swallowing, and the disease has caused painful contractures and akathisia: he is constantly restless and agitated; his body can't stop moving. He pedals and kicks and stretches and sits up and lies down. He says to me in what remains of his whispering voice, "I'm done with all this. There's no point in living." He gestures vaguely. "I want it here," he adds, pointing to his chest, "D. N. R." He is done. Is he depressed? Would you be?

As death approaches, as social roles fall away and the body's needs begin to require most of your attention, your focus narrows. You may be thinking about the seemingly endless losses, your ever-increasing need for help, your fear and worries. Or you may be homing in on the meaning, reflecting on the past, attending to the changes every day brings. Dying is psychological work, emotional work, spiritual work. The simplest things take time; everything once taken for granted changes, and a person either gets sad or gets mad or settles into a new kind of peace. Sometimes the question is just *Why?* Not *Why now? Why her? Why me?* or *Why so soon?* but *Why? Why death? Why an end to life? Why a mystery?* The search for the answer may be called religion, science, philosophy, or something else entirely. Those who find a satisfying answer often find it difficult to explain. But no matter what we call this quest, the search for the why of death is one for the individual to

undertake. Never bring your private beliefs about death to someone else's deathbed. Together we collude in denial or aversion;
alone we may find a way out.

To find meaning is to make sense of things, and the meaning of
your death will not be the meaning of mine. As death approaches,
one's entire life can become coherent and whole. But the questions may remain and may never be answered: *Who am I now? Why
is this happening?* You may seek a higher order of things in which a
human life fits. You may seek a reason, an explanation, some clue
that your death makes sense. It may be salvation or a matter of
entropy. You may seek to know *why*, above all.

A man named John Shields died in Canada last year. Shields
had a painful, debilitating disease and chose medical assistance
in dying in the first months after the controversial Canadian law
passed. He wanted to make his decision to die deliberately in front
of others, in the hopes that his death could help other people. He
had been a priest, a social worker, a union activist, an environmental leader; his entire life had been about helping people. In his
final days, he had a vivid dream of sweeping up broken glass from
a hallway, so that it would be safe for other people to walk.

6

Where?

Until the 1930s, most people in the United States died at home. Today about 80 percent of American deaths and almost as many in the United Kingdom take place in hospitals or nursing homes.

We usually have no choice about when we die, so if we can, we try to choose where we die. The rise of hospice services has brought back the idea of dying at home. Here's that pretty picture again: Grandpa in his own bed, surrounded by loving family. But home is more complicated than you think, and often a mixed blessing at best.

Dying at home, with loving but untrained family who may not understand how to read distressing changes or use medicines properly, may be more uncomfortable than in the supposedly sterile atmosphere of an institution. The extended families and stay-at-home parents of the 1930s have disappeared into a maze of apartment complexes, long commutes, and extra shifts. This is one reason why poor people are more likely to die in a hospital than rich people. Our image of Grandpa at home in his own bed assumes that Grandpa likes his bed, that his house is safe and quiet, and that he really wants his relatives to take care of his most personal needs. He may actually want the professional attention, twenty-four-hour care, and security that a hospital provides. He may want no part of the sticky attempts at "closure" and exhortations for self-reflection that eager caregivers may bring. Hospitals are controlled environments and may feel safer to a fragile person than a house at the end of a long road or an apartment in a large complex of strangers. You can have a bad death in your own bed and a good death in an ICU.

If you are going to try to take care of a dying person at home, ask yourself who *can* help. Some people can't do it. They disappear. They don't say goodbye, answer calls, write letters. The whole family heads for the hills. (They call now and then, perhaps with advice or complaints or needs of their own.) In many families, one person becomes the primary caregiver. Or the only caregiver. On the one hand, this is abandonment; on the other, it is self-defense. Some people can't do it; they can't bear it; they would be no good if they tried. If you are the caregiver left behind, beware the simmer of resentment. Holding a grudge for any length of time is more damaging to you than to anyone else. If someone disappears at the critical juncture, it is their loss, and they may, in fact, be doing the best they can with what seems like an impossible situation. Yes, it's awful for one child or sibling to carry the load. It's awful for you; it's awful for the others, too: they know they are missing something important. Meanwhile, you will have to fill the gap.

Presuming people are willing to help, and those willing are in fact physically, emotionally, and mentally capable of providing good care—and they feel able to provide the most intimate of physical care to, say, a parent or sibling—how much *can* people help? Who can get the time off work, away from child care? Who can stay through the night? Who can help you lift?

Deaths can destroy families. They are often shattering events, and not every relationship among survivors will last. A family is a dance, a web, a delicately balanced tower of fine porcelain. When a person leaves the dance, partners change, steps are forgotten, and we are not even sure who is leading anymore. No crisis can knock down the building blocks of adulthood faster. Your brother turns into the bullying eight-year-old who tickled you until you cried. Your aunt announces to your mother, *I'm going to kill myself when you die.* Your cousin appears out of the blue and loudly tells everyone that the dying person promised him a bequest, to which your sister replies, *That drop-leaf table is mine. Take a hike.* And you, you're thinking, *Help!*

Until a death is right in the middle of the family web, its members may not grasp what *dependency* means, what *caregiving* means, what loss and grieving do to the thick, confused agreements between members. Until it happens, you don't know what is going to be easy to do. You don't know what will prove to be just too hard to do at all. Sometimes the missing relatives show up just in time to insist that everything be done differently, that's not what she would have wanted, how could you make that decision without me?

The amount of what is known as "bedside care" required by a dying patient is more than a challenge to untrained caregivers. How will you handle confusion or agitation in the middle of the night? What will you do if a person falls? What happens if there is bleeding? Can you change the clothing or the bed linens if a person throws up or has diarrhea? Are you prepared to stay awake all night?

Dying people often need a hospital bed. In many homes, that means he will be limited to the living room. There will be no privacy. If he needs a wheelchair, the doorways may not be wide enough. He will need a shower chair and guardrails if he can get to the bathroom. If he can't get into the bathroom, he will need a commode. In the living room. If he can't stand, he may need a mechanical lift. Such lifts are large and cumbersome and simply don't fit in many rooms, especially with a hospital bed. The alternative to a lift is being confined to bed or being lifted by several strong people. Will several strong people be there when you need them?

I've worked in an excellent palliative care program for about ten years. About a fifth of our clients die every year. They are frail people with complicated medical needs, whether from age or illness or both. They need a lot of attention and we know them well. Few of my clients live in the family home; they need too much care for too long. I am used to deaths in which people have had a chance to plan ahead and make decisions, their symptoms are managed as well as possible, good bedside care is given, nurses visit regularly, and their families are supported and informed. The majority of deaths I see are anticipated and carefully attended, and I am confident that most of these are "good" deaths by any definition of the word. I've seen good deaths in foster care and assisted living and a retirement center and a skilled nursing home, and occasionally in the hospital—that is, places built with dependent people in mind, and trained caregivers available around the clock. I tend to forget that a lot of deaths are not like this for the simple reason that people are not getting good nursing and medical care by experienced providers.

But, you cry in dismay, *we have hospice!* About 40 percent of Americans have hospice services when they die. What that oft-cited statistic actually means is that 40 percent of Americans have had at least *three days* of service. Three days. The median length of time in hospice is only seventeen days.

When people think of a hospice, they are often thinking of what are called "freestanding" hospices: a special place you go to, to be cared for when you die. Only a few hospices are like this. A few are dedicated hospital units. "Home hospice," in which the patient is cared for at home, accounts for 94 percent of hospice services in the United States. In the last fifteen years, the number of hospices in the US has almost doubled, and this increase is largely represented by for-profit corporations. Hospice for profit is a concept that many people find incongruous—or offensive. Almost one in five people admitted to a hospice are discharged from hospice *before* dying, often with only two days' notice. The hospices with the highest rate for doing this have the highest profits. Federal regulators have raised the question of whether hospices are admitting people who really aren't as sick as they are supposed to be and discharging a patient when, for whatever reason, she needs a hospital stay.

The criterion for entering hospice is often casually defined as "no one will be surprised if he is dead in six months." In fact, there is a detailed algorithm of clinical signs and symptoms, and both a primary doctor and the hospice doctor have to certify a person's eligibility. Some signs are universal and others are specific to an illness like cancer, Alzheimer's disease, or HIV/AIDS. For instance, hospice criteria for pulmonary disease includes a "disabling dyspnea at rest; poor response to bronchodilators; pO2 below 55 mm Hg" and several other factors. What if you're just very old? If you're over eighty years old, most people won't be surprised if you're dead in six months. But an eighty-year-old may not have the clinical markers of organ failure needed for hospice.

The Medicare benefit for hospice requires people to give up treatments aimed at curing the terminal illness, and some may not admit people who want to receive purely supportive treatments like blood transfusions. This is one reason black Americans use hospice less often than white Americans. One of the most important reasons for the difference is the long history of inadequate and discriminatory medical treatment they've experienced; if you've been abused by the health care system for generations, it can be hard to trust any advice that implies less treatment. Far fewer black Americans have advance directives than white Americans, and they are more likely than white Americans to insist on advanced life support and resuscitation even in the face of terminal illness, often because of religious beliefs about the redemptive power of suffering and the importance of trusting that God can work miracles. To many black Christians, accepting hospice or signing an advance directive seems disrespectful to God. (A black minister who works in palliative care and is trying to overcome this resistance says, "What I don't think they realize is that when they pray for a healing, death is a healing. . . . It's not the healing that you might want, but as sure as we're born, we're going to die. And we're healed from the troubles of this world.")

Hospice doesn't provide primary care; it covers help with the terminal illness and nothing else. You need another doctor (and insurance) for other problems, from migraines to asthma. Many hospices want the primary doctor to manage the symptoms of the terminal illness as well. Hospice only pays for medications needed for pain relief and the symptoms of the terminal illness. Hospice doesn't pay for an ambulance or a trip to an emergency room without prior approval.

This stark separation of care can lead to real problems. Very few people have a single terminal illness and no other complaints.

What if the most uncomfortable problem you have is arthritis? What if you need medications, a walker, and physical therapy to help with the arthritis while you die from a painless form of cancer? It happens. What if you are slowly dying from cancer and suddenly develop a curable problem that is making your life miserable and requires a hospital stay—say, kidney stones?

Hospice can be wonderful, providing reassurance, guidance, and support to both the dying and their family. But hospice can be woefully inadequate. Home hospice has to offer one visit from a nurse per week, and two visits from a nursing aide in a week, "up to 90 minutes" in length. In other words, about four hours of face-to-face care in a week; how much help you get in a crisis outside business hours may be dependent on "staffing levels." A friend of our family lived alone in what is called a "single-occupancy" building: a room with a bathroom down the hall. He had hospice services. But even as he deteriorated badly and became unable to eat or go to the bathroom alone—even as he had uncontrolled pain—the hospice service didn't send help or suggest that he needed more care somewhere else. It was, after all, a home hospice service. After he moved in with us, we saw a nurse for two brief visits, and no one else at all. I had gotten the hospital bed myself from another company.

The explicit intention of hospice is for your family to take care of you. The Medicare information packet explains, "Hospice benefit allows you and your family to stay together in the comfort of your home." A few studies show that the majority of families are grateful for hospice services. A lot of anecdotal stories report the opposite. In part, dissatisfaction is the result of inaccurate expectations. People believe, and in many cases are led to believe, that hospice care means *caregiving*. That's not what hospice services do. In some cases, the family is required to guarantee that a patient will never be left alone. Respite care, in which the family is given a chance to rest for a few hours or days, may or may not be available.

"You and your family are the most important part of a team." But the interests of the patient and family may conflict. What if a patient wants hospice care and the family doesn't want to provide it? Or wants to and simply can't? Patient and family may have very different interests and hopes for the death. Any conflict between the wishes of the patient and the wishes of the family providing care is not going to go the patient's way. The conflict may not even be between the patient and his family members but among the family members themselves. If one relative is the designated representative, she may need to hold that responsibility in the face of terrible accusations and arguments.

Palliative care is the specialty focused on comfort and quality of life in people with chronic and terminal illness, even while you seek a cure, even if you have come to terms with dying. (The cartoonist Roz Chast proposes "*extreme* palliative care," which she thinks could include all-you-can-eat ice cream parlors and heroin.) I wear my bias on my sleeve. I believe in palliative care for anyone with a serious illness, and I know that palliative care can provide the support needed for a good death. Yet palliative care receives a laughably tiny fraction of the money spent on medical care.

One of the good physicians with whom I work keeps a cartoon on her office door. The doctor is talking to the patient, gowned and barefoot, sitting on the exam table: "You've got six months. But with aggressive treatment, we can help make that seem much longer." No system is perfect, but a good palliative care program can make an enormous difference in a person's life and death. The care given is interdisciplinary, which means that alongside the doctor and nurse may be social workers, chaplains, and physical, occupational, and speech therapists. Palliative care is concerned with everything that affects the quality of a person's life, which might include treating the headache and going to the emergency room with a sprained ankle. This is all offered while you cope with cancer or heart disease or whatever brought you there. It may include help with bathing, visits to the eye doctor and the dentist, equipment like hearing aids and orthopedic shoes and walkers, recreational and respite programs, and visits to specialists.

Palliative care has a broad scope. Programs can be specific—for people in treatment for cancer—or general, for anyone with a chronic illness. A person in liver failure may benefit greatly from it while waiting for the transplant that will cure the liver failure. Cancer patients getting chemotherapy do better in treatment with palliative care because the team can help with symptoms. A program may offer acupuncture, help solve financial issues, sort out family dynamics, and design an exercise program—all while the person is trying to get better. My immense textbook calls this "active total care." You can have palliative care while you're trying to live, and you can have palliative care until the last hour of your life.

Medicine focuses on cures, because a cure is often possible. But once upon a time, comfort was a central part of medicine. Modern medical practice is still sorting out the fact that not doing something is a medical act, and good medicine may mean stopping what you are doing. Really good medicine is more concerned with how a patient feels about her life—and death—than anything else. Lindy West sat at her father's bedside as he was dying of cancer.

He had been unconscious for days. A doctor came in now and then and asked how the family was doing. *Terrible,* she thought. *What do you think?* "Is there anything we can do?" the doctor would then ask. West thought: "Apparently not, considering this whole long-slow-death thing that's happening in this room right now. Also, you're the doctor. You tell me."

To provide a good death, the caregivers must do *for* the patient, not *to* the patient. She is not a disease or a collection of symptoms or a problem needing a solution. Any doctor who approaches the terminally ill person with the idea that he or she is in charge is on the wrong track. I was really annoyed by an essay by an obviously young neurologist who wrote that hospice doctors are "the artists of death." No, my friend. The dying person is the artist of his or her death. And that death started a long time before you came into the room, and it will continue when you aren't around, and it will endure long after you've made your pronouncement.

Occasionally, I have to make the hard call to a family member. This is something a person learns to do in all the worst ways: by making mistakes. By saying the wrong thing. I've done that, and I've learned. I break the news differently, depending on the situation, on whether I know the person I'm talking to, whether I know there is unusual stress in the family. I speak differently to the daughter who visits every day than I might to the sister who lives across the country. I usually start by saying I have some serious news about their relative. If things have just suddenly changed, I might use the phrase *final illness* or *last hours* or I may simply say, "She's dying." Then I add—almost always, because this is almost always true—"She looks very comfortable. She is quiet. She seems peaceful." Because on the other end of the phone is a son or daughter or sister or husband hurrying to find the car keys or turn off the stove, and not able to take in much more at that point. *How long? How soon? Now?* If I have to tell someone that their relative has died—which in many cases is not a surprise and may be a great relief—I start the same way. Serious news.

I've seen good doctors stumble over what is called bad news. I've seen doctors looming over fragile patients in wheelchairs, speaking in jargon and interrupting the person's questions. Doctors forget that anxiety makes it hard to remember details and that a person getting this bad news doesn't know the Latin words or our internal shorthand for treatments. I've seen a doctor shake the hand of a person she's never met before and plunge directly into a technical discussion of whether or not the person would like to be resuscitated in the event that he stops breathing.

When I worked on the oncology unit, an elderly woman spent the evening with her husband and then left to drive home. About ten minutes after she left, her husband had a cardiac arrest. He didn't survive, even with aggressive efforts. I was his primary nurse, so it was up to me to call his wife. I simply told her that he had taken a turn for the worse and that she should return as soon as possible. When she reached the unit, obviously distressed, I took her into a private room where the cardiologist who had led the resuscitation attempt waited. He stood over her and began describing the anatomy of the heart's circulatory system.

Finally, she turned to me and said, "What is he talking about?" The cardiologist said nothing, and it was left to me to tell her that her husband was dead.

Another evening, a doctor walked out of a patient's room saying to me, "You tell him," and what I was to tell him was that he would have to choose between going on a ventilator that night and never coming off, or dying. That night.

You can fire your doctor. I am surprised at how many people think this isn't possible—that the doctor is in charge, the boss of you, the only authority. But you are the authority of your own life, and the doctor works for you. How do you fire your doctor? "Doctor, you're fired." A good doctor is going to want to know what he did to upset you; if he doesn't ask, consider it proof that you made the right choice. In a large hospital, a staff doctor called a hospitalist may be able to take over your care while you look for a new primary doctor. You may be able to switch to one of your former doctor's partners, or you may need to move to another office.

So. It's time to buy the farm. Pay the piper. If you want to die at home, get all the help you can. Get help from the neighbors and friends and your church and the veterans' organization and the AA group and your model train hobby association. Get everybody. Then get a good hospice or palliative care program involved, and insist on getting what you are promised. Read the fine print.

If the dice rolls a certain way, you may die in a hospital. This can happen for any number of reasons, and it doesn't mean failure. It doesn't mean you or your caregivers did anything wrong, missed a trick, made a mistake. Sometimes a dying person's needs can only be met in a hospital. We tend to think of hospitals as places where crises are unfolding, and the halls are noisy and nights are broken. But that is only part of it. Many parts of hospitals are hushed and warm; the pace is deliberate rather than hurried; the staff is attentive and skilled. If you get the right hospital at the very end of your life, you'll have a private room; you can bring in photographs and music; you can have your own pillow. Nurses will offer to shut your door and will knock before entering and never leave without asking, "Is there anything else I can do?" The staff will help you manage visitors and be the gatekeeper and the bouncer if you need one. (Most hospitals have a system where you can keep the fact that you are a patient there completely private, or use a code word so that only certain people are given news.) You will be on a firm but comfortable mattress, with no plastic under your skin. No machines will start beeping just when you're falling asleep. No alarms will ring. No one will wake you up to take a sleeping pill. You can wear your favorite pajamas.

There are plenty of hospital units where the nurses know exactly how to take care of dying people and the hospitalists know the right medication to order and will lean against the window ledge and answer all your questions patiently. There are hospitals where the staff will leave you alone with your vigilant loved ones when you are actually dying, like the hospital where I was born and my mother quietly died, thirty years later, with her family in a private room. They will leave you alone because the people in the room have been told what's happening and what's normal and when to call for help. This hospital may not be a hospital at all. It could be a freestanding hospice or a palliative care unit or a skilled nursing home or a retirement center or even your family home with all the help you need. This is not a fantasy. I've worked in a hospital like this. I've been the nurse in rooms like this—and I always knock before I enter.

While you're getting ready to kick that bucket and head for room temperature, we'll tell jokes if you like. When you're about to check into the Motel Deep 6, the coffeepot will be fresh and the muffins full of butter. All of this is possible, but a lot of it happens because you insist. Because you and I and all the rest of us insist that there are enough chairs for everyone, that the curtains will close tightly when you want to sleep, and the room will smell fresh and sweet.

And you will be comfortable, because in the good hospital your pain medication comes on time and the nurse who brings it knows how to read dying, knows what's to be expected and what can be fixed and what can't. In the good hospital, strong hands will clean you up when you can't make it to the toilet any longer and no one will make a face or say things that are better not said as you shuffle off the mortal coil. What a wonderful turn of phrase that is. When you're ready for your dirt nap and you've bought your one-way ticket, the nurses will take their time. They won't rush. They will come in quietly and wash you carefully and brush your hair and clean up and slip away again.

7

Last Weeks

Dying can be boring; the world narrows until it seems no larger than the room. But most of the time we forget the *intensity* of it. Everyone is filled with emotion, moving as though through pudding. One person feels muted. Another presses his hand against his chest to ease the heartache. One visitor is sober; another can't stop laughing. The whole situation is impossible. You are filled with panic at times. You are shattered. You will feel . . . everything.

Dying is messy, too—bodies and minds, plans, relationships. A crowd of people passes through, bringing flowers and leaving dirty dishes and footprints. So you spend hours washing dishes and mopping while the cheap flowers in the cheap vases drop petals all over the floor. The laundry piles up, the bills aren't paid, and no one wants to take out the garbage. You feel afraid. You feel guilty about being afraid. You feel angry. You feel guilty about being angry. You feel grateful for every hour remaining. You feel horrible, because you are longing for the death to come so that all this will be over. You feel tenderness so deep your skin seems transparent.

I took the Death Attitude Profile (Revised). The creators

of the DAP-R were psychologists who believed that when it came to our ideas about death, "fear and acceptance coexist in an uneasy truce." The DAP-R was created to distinguish a person's fear of death—which may drive him to reflect and seek meaning—from a complete avoidance of thinking about death, which can interfere with any search for meaning. There are many such tools, though I am not at all convinced of their usefulness. Do we *need* to take a questionnaire to know how we feel about death? Do we need to score our beliefs in order to know whether we are scared or not? If we're intent on avoiding thinking about death, how many of these questionnaires are we willing to take?

I decided to find out what I could discover, and I was determined to be honest even if that meant admitting to feelings I didn't want to have. The profile is a set of thirty-two questions, such as: "I am disturbed by the finality of death," "Death is no doubt a grim experience," "Death is a deliverance from pain and suffering," and "I see death as a passage to an eternal and blessed place." In each case, I was asked if I *strongly agree, agree, moderately agree, moderately disagree, disagree, strongly disagree,* or if I was undecided. I tried—I really did—but I found the test impossible to translate to my own belief system. My score was all over the place, internally contradictory, a failure of epistemological translation. Where in these questions does this belief fit? "All compounded things are subject to dissolution." This formula is basic Buddhist doctrine, poured into me by the canon, by my teachers, by my daily life. All things are compounded and will dissolve, which means *I* am compounded and *I* will dissolve. This is not something I readily accept, and yet I am continually bombarded with the evidence. I longed to understand this fact of life, this answer to a question I didn't learn how to ask for a long time. But does it mean that I see death as something grim? Or a passage to a blessed place? No and no.

François Rabelais was a sixteenth-century physician and writer and a most unusual priest—a questing humanist in an orthodox world. He died at the age of fifty-nine with the supposed last words: "I am going in search of a great perhaps." Perhaps. Perhaps we fear extinction; perhaps we are doing our best at terror management. Perhaps we can hardly wait for what is overtly called the promised land. There are many forms of consolation, and many pathways of fear. Part of getting ready to die is looking at one's innermost beliefs: faith, goodness, sin, regret, reward, metaphysical power, and very private doubts. Looking directly at a topic we may have tried not to look at our entire lives: what happens next. Epicurus insisted that we cannot ever know; there will be no one present to find out. An "I" knows that the "I" will cease to be. What "I" will be left to do whatever is to be done?

The lovely Japanese film called *After Life* is a fable about where people go right after they die; it turns out to be a run-down hotel in the country. People arrive one by one, a little disoriented. Each person is given a room and told that they can stay until they pick a single memory in which to live forever. Once they pick the memory, the staff re-creates it and the person settles in and disappears. Some people choose immediately and happily fade away. Another person spends days reviewing the jerky black-and-white films of his life, trying to pick one. A few people have no happy memories and just sit on their beds, lost. A few others find it impossible to decide: their lives are full. (One of the key parts of the plot is what happens to the ones who can't decide.)

When I showed *After Life* to a group of people, we did what every viewer will do, and thought about which memory we would choose. I was struck by the common thread, for me and for many people: it was the moment after. Not the adventure, the experience, the fulfilled desire, but afterward. The moment of tired satisfaction, of knowing one is satisfied. The moment at the end of a good day when you are going home and are a little sore and sweaty, you are getting hungry, your feet are dirty, and you are going home to rest.

I heard a woman talking about her need to make decisions, as she was expected to die soon. Her friend asked her how she was going to do that, how she would decide.

"I don't know," she said, with a little wonder. "I've never done this before—at least, not that I remember." Have we? Do we know how? Maybe it's built into the organism; call it collective memory, call it a genetic trait, call it rebirth. People often seem to know the way, to remember as though dying were a skill they learned a long time ago and haven't used in many years. But they remember. It is not entirely new.

"How long?" This urgent question can't be answered. Not exactly. The *BMJ* (formerly the *British Medical Journal*) looked at the predictions of survival made by physicians for 1,500 people with cancer. The doctors often overestimated survival times. (Research shows that doctors, and to some extent nurses, are overly optimistic about medical treatment in general.) Prognosis is a prediction of how long a person will be sick, or how long he will live, and it does get more accurate as a person draws closer to death. No one can unfailingly predict how and when the body will finally fail.

Death makes itself known like the breeze makes itself known to the mobile: every piece begins to move, and the movement of one arm pulls on another, which bounces against another until every part is slowly spinning even after the breeze has passed. The body is unfathomably complex and entangled. Bodies are unique. Every disease manifests differently from one body to the next. And yet, the closer death comes, the more universal the body seems to be, the more familiar the signs, until it becomes like walking down a street you know well.

There is always a last time. The last walk, and then the last time you walk at all. The last time you shower by yourself, and then the last time you have a shower. The last time you eat steak, and then the last time you eat solid food.

The last time you go fishing.

I met Butch when my husband became his AA sponsor, and he came to our house for Thanksgiving. It was his first family Thanksgiving dinner in decades—maybe in his life. Butch had been in prison for armed robbery for nearly thirty years. His brutal and abusive childhood gave way to a wild adolescence, drugs and crime, and finally prison. His new life out of prison was the difficult life of the ex-con, to whom we give nothing but obstacles. He was getting old, but he couldn't get Social Security because he'd been in prison his entire adult life and hadn't paid into the system. He didn't qualify for most services. Finally, he found a job working for a local agency helping homeless people, many of whom were also former inmates. The job gave him enough for a little room of his own where he could have a cat—a white cat named Cleo. A room of his own, with a window. A cat to hold. A fishing pole.

What he really wanted to do was fish. Every day he could, he would get up at four in the morning, walk to the bus station with his fishing gear, and take the first bus of the day all the way to the end of the line. Then he walked two miles to a lake where he could fish alone in the sunlight as long as he wanted. Butch was glad to be free and glad to be sober, and he loved the sun. Nothing was easy, but it was his.

A few years after his release, Butch was diagnosed with liver cancer. He quietly refused help; he was doing fine, he didn't need anything, thanks. But things got too hard. At last he was accepted into a home hospice program while we waited through the enrollment period for the agency where I worked. But he was already in too much trouble. A hospice nurse dropped by now and then but seemed oblivious to his struggles: the lack of food, the fact that he could not always get to the bathroom in time, that he was in pain.

It took a few tries, but my husband finally convinced Butch to come and stay at our house. By then he was unsteady and a little confused. He came with a small bag and his cat, and sat dozing on the couch while a couple of men unloaded a hospital bed and set it up in the living room. I made sure he was facing the window. From then on, he slept a lot, with Cleo curled up on the foot of the bed. He tottered to the commode, smiled, but said little. A steady stream of men came to sit with him, men who had also been in prison and struggled with drugs, and knew him from the homeless shelter and the downtown AA meetings. They were disheveled, polite, mostly sober. They smoked out on the sidewalk in small groups, sat on the porch steps, took turns holding Butch's hand or helping him to take a sip of water. Sometimes they prayed or held an impromptu twelve-step meeting. One young man asked if he could take the night shift, and he moved in, too, and slept on the floor in the kitchen so he could hear Butch call if he needed anything.

In the last weeks, fatigue is profound. Everything is fading, energy leaking away. In a profound way, this *is* how we die, this *is* death, the utter dissipation of energy. If you want to help, do the small things that seem as though they should be easy but are not. A person may want to finish a few chores, as much to spare the living from the work as for her own wish for it to be done. People need to tie things up. To finish. (I think of that moment after the adventure ends—that tired satisfaction.) Help to write letters or wrap gifts. If her most avid wish is to finally get the hall closet organized, get cracking. She can't do it by herself anymore.

You can also remember skin. Fatigue means she is spending a lot of time in bed or curled in the same chair. She may not move for hours, and she has lost weight. The skin is a thin and friable organ now. In old age, skin can become paper-thin, and it can tear like paper. Pressure is dangerous. Remind her to change position. Help her to change position. If you are helping with personal care, watch for areas of redness that won't go away, especially over what are called the bony prominences: hips and heels, knees and elbows, the tailbone, shoulder blades, and vertebrae. Gentle massage can be good, a real help now, but you have to be careful. Any injury or sore on the skin should be reported to the nurse immediately.

Breath. Breathing. On and on, we breathe. When people have difficulty breathing, our own breath will catch in a kind of organic fright. A condition called dyspnea, sometimes simply known as difficult breathing, often happens toward the end of life. This may be related to a disease process like chronic emphysema, or just the body's failing strength. It may be worse with activity or emotional distress. Unsurprisingly, dyspnea often includes anxiety, restlessness, a feeling of tightness in the chest, and sometimes panic or dread. There may be no clinical signs—no change in oxygen levels or blood pressure or heart rate. A person may look relaxed and still feel breathless, what is called "air hunger," when every breath feels inadequate.

Dyspnea should be evaluated by the nurse and medical provider to determine if there is a cause other than the dying process, because several causes of dyspnea can be treated. People assume oxygen will fix it, but dyspnea often doesn't change oxygen levels in the blood. A lack of oxygen is not the problem, and it should be used only if it genuinely makes the person feel better. Lots of people find oxygen annoying. Nasal cannulas and masks are uncomfortable and interfere with physical intimacy. Oxygen can cause dry mouth and even nosebleeds. Unless the person has abnormally low levels of oxygen in their bloodstream, oxygen is simply an unpleasant intrusion. Is the oxygen just making the caregivers and family feel better—feel like they are doing *something*?

There are lots of other things to do to make breathing more comfortable. Pursed-lip breathing is efficient and can relieve the struggle. Simply purse your lips as though about to whistle while you breathe through your mouth. Breathe *with* the person: regular, even breaths. If a person is anxious and gasping, breathe slowly and deeply with him for a few minutes. Place a fan or open a window to allow cool air to blow gently across the person's cheek. The reason this works is unclear, though it may be a stimulation of one of the cranial nerves affecting the respiratory center. It may simply be a psychological trick, a reminder that there is air available. Provide space around the bed and chair so that the person does not feel crowded, and raise the head of the bed a little. A person may be more comfortable leaning forward with their arms on a table or pillow. Finally, morphine often helps; no one knows exactly why.

People eat and drink less, and eventually will stop altogether. Even a person with severe dementia who needs to be spoon-fed will stop turning toward the spoon, stop opening his mouth. Most dying people don't choose to quit eating and drinking; they simply cease wanting to. The point comes when a dying person is unable to eat or drink. Food and water keep us alive; hunger and thirst are the reflexes of a living body, meeting the needs of a healthy body. Turning away from what is no longer needed is part of dying.

Digestion is slowing down and the kidneys are becoming less efficient. A dying person simply is unable to digest food like a healthy one, and becomes much less able to manage fluids. The ability to swallow begins to fade, and choking becomes a concern. *Do not force food or fluids.* Instead of fretting about calories, help them brush their teeth or suck on a moist washcloth. If a person is not drinking, the family may want intravenous fluids. Needles are uncomfortable in the best of circumstances, and as a person fails, it will be difficult to start a line. The tubing is often in the way, especially if a person is restless or needing frequent changes. What is it—who is it—you really want to feed? Does it feel like neglect not to insist that a person eat? Nothing is being withheld. Instead, you are no longer forcing food and fluid on a person who is neither interested nor able to take it. A person who doesn't want to eat may seem like a person who doesn't want to live. Remember that wanting has nothing to do with it.

If you are with a person who is dying, you will see them shrink: not just with lost weight but into a kind of gauntness that seems in part metaphysical, a stepping out of things. They are shrinking out of life. I get thirsty; you get thirsty—isn't the person in bed thirsty? Aren't they hungry? Probably not. I know it's hard to believe, but not eating and drinking may actually make people more comfortable. Dying people do experience thirst sometimes, but water and fluids don't relieve it. This peculiar thirst seems to be a symptom of dying. Nurses and doctors can recount endless stories of people who have no food or fluid at all for a week or more, who never express thirst or pain, and have a peaceful death. People who are clinically dehydrated sometimes live longer than people getting intravenous fluids.

Why is a state of dehydration a boon? The person may be nauseated or have pain or difficulty breathing whenever they try to eat (and as appetite ceases, she may be trying to eat only to please her anxious caregivers). The kidneys and heart become less able to manage extra fluid. Water accumulates in tissues and the abdominal cavity, causing painful swelling and edema. Dehydration can partly reverse these conditions and reduce swelling around tumors as well, decreasing pain. The fact is just that after being allowed to stop eating and drinking, people often perk up. They feel better, and they die more peacefully.

A special note on artificial feeding, also known as tube feeding. If a person cannot swallow, a tube can be surgically inserted into the stomach for liquid nutrition and medications. For a person with a neurological disorder affecting swallowing, this can be a lifesaver. After certain surgeries, tube feeding is a good temporary treatment. For a person who is dying, it is a special kind of torture. Tube feeding has many complications, including pain, infections, and ulcers. But even if it were without side effects, artificial feeding is futile. It won't cure anything, and may not prolong life—but if it does, it is prolonging a life that is trying to end. There is a reason that every advance directive specifically addresses tube feeding.

A certain number of people in a slow decline consciously choose to stop eating and drinking. The medical term for this is "voluntary dehydration," but there is no need to turn this into a clinical issue. Many cultures support the idea of fasting as a religious practice, as a way to focus the mind, and as a way to prepare for death. Even without religious intent, a conscious person may say it is just time not to eat anymore. Eventually, he no longer wants even water.

Scott Nearing—peace activist, writer, radical economist, and passionate advocate of a simple life—often said he wanted to live to be ninety-nine years old. He did, and toward the end of that year, he was watching his wife, Helen, eat. He told her, she recalled, "I think I won't eat anymore." She said, "I understand. I think I would do that too. Animals know when to stop. They go off in a corner and leave off food." Helen started offering him juice: "carrot juice, apple juice, banana juice, pineapple, grape— any kind. I kept him full of liquids as often as he was thirsty. He got weaker, of course, and he was as gaunt and thin as Gandhi. Came a day he said, 'I think I'll go on water. Nothing more.' From then on, for about ten days, he only had water.

"He was bed-ridden and had little strength but spoke with me daily. In the morning of August 24, 1983, two weeks after his 100th birthday, when it seemed he was slipping away, I sat beside him on his bed. We were quiet together; no interruptions, no doctors or hospitals. I said 'It's alright, Scott. Go right along.'" And then, "with no quiver or pain or disturbance he said 'All . . . right,' and breathed slower and slower and slower till there was no movement anymore and he was gone out of his body as easily as a leaf drops from the tree in autumn, slowly twisting and falling to the ground."

Hello, caregiver: you are so tired. You need time to be alone, even if it's just in a corner of the house where you can rest, or a chance to go to a coffee shop for an hour or two. You need time to talk to someone else, about other things, in another room. The dying person may not want to talk anymore, may not want you near, but he doesn't want to be alone. You can't leave. What you need most is all the help you can get. Ask for it. Accept it. Night may be the scariest time: long, spooky hours filled with questions. Night, when you are the most worn and just want to be home or need to be caring for children and doing laundry and getting ready for work—this is when the person needs you the most. They need you to be there, and they need you to be willing to be silent or talk or listen or read out loud or stand vigil. They need you to be ready. Get help, so that you can be.

Here at the threshold, one has trouble finding solid ground. The world is as shaky as a crumbling cliff at times, as still as the bottom of a well at others. Kate Carroll de Gutes took care of her mother through a years-long marathon of dementia, moving, surgery, unhealing wounds, and intensive care units, until her mother finally began to die. And then Kate took care of her while she died.

"Death is like this: it's exhausting is what it is," she wrote. "Everything feels like a huge fucking emergency. Why is that brown Camry torturing me by driving two miles per hour under the speed limit? Why did the Union Cab taxi dispatcher take thirty minutes to call me back to tell me the cab wasn't coming? Why! Is! The! God! Damned! Internet! So! Slow!" She couldn't describe what she was feeling for a long time. "I didn't understand how the liminal space that the dying person is in can affect your own psyche." She got lost driving home, forgot appointments, even forgot her age. ("Was I twenty-one or forty-one? Was I here or there?")

Everything alters; time stretches and recedes; nothing happens. Suddenly a lot seems to be happening. Then nothing happens again. Dying is like this: we walk together down the road, side by side, or one leading the other, until the road diverges into two. We stand there for a while together, waiting. Then a person turns to walk down one path while the rest of us head down the other. We watch her go. We wave, we call out her name, but she doesn't look back. The time comes when the dying person doesn't want to chat about the news or the kids or your job. There is nothing else anymore but this solitary walk.

Kate gradually learned how to be in that world, the incomparable world of a dying person, and she learned this the way a graduate student in a really difficult master's program learns a new vocabulary, a new skill set, and a new identity. She says of people caring for the dying, "We are confused, and in our confusion we are finally able to see clearly and sing out in our full range." We sing out goodbye.

Death takes many forms. One death is anticipated over months. Another death is stunningly abrupt. And now and then death is held back by technology. I have seen how these deaths are different, and they are all the same, in the end: a person breathes and then breathes no more. He enters a stillness like no other. Breath. Another breath, and then no more. But when the breaths are made by a machine or the blood pressure is sustained by powerful drugs, someone has to make an awful decision.

Many aspects of medical and nursing care become unnecessary or intrusive for a dying person. Will the result of a lab test change the plan? If not, then don't do it. Why take another vitamin? Are you really worried about the cholesterol level at this point? You don't need to check blood pressure routinely. But sometimes a person is already hooked up—intravenous fluids and drugs to raise blood pressure and support for breathing—and the only way to stop the intrusion is to unhook. The advent of machines like defibrillators and ventilators created a new kind of crisis for the dying. (One report from the time referred to "this era of resuscitatory arrogance.") A lecture in 1967 about how medicine should define death was called "The Right to Be Let Alone."

Futility is a legal term in health care. A doctor, a team of people, even a hospital, can invoke futility and refuse to continue treatment that only prolongs suffering. This doesn't happen immediately; it's a drawn-out, painful process. The vocabulary makes everything worse. Doctors speak almost glibly about "withdrawing" or "withholding" treatment. The nurse says, "There's nothing more to be done." Which is a stupid thing to say, because there are all kinds of things to be done; they just don't involve trying to keep someone alive. Such comments create a terrible sense of culpability in a heartbroken spouse or child. But what is really being done is good care.

Virginia Morris pleads for a change of terms: "When we take a terminally ill patient off life support, we are not 'pulling the plug,' we are 'freeing' the patient to die. We are 'releasing' her from excessive technology and invasive treatments. When we allow death to happen, we are not killing people, we are caring for them. We are loving them."

We want to put it off as long as possible. Even if we are sure that Mom or Dad wouldn't want to be kept alive "on a machine," in the moment of crisis when everyone is yelling at us to decide, we're not prepared. We literally have no experience making such a decision; we may do it only once in our lives.

The hardest part is the loss, but a close second is the need to shove your own fears and desires to the side. Sherwin Nuland said that at the time when decisions about life support and life-prolonging treatments are being made, "everybody becomes enormously selfish." He emphatically includes doctors and nurses in with the family. We may not recognize that selfishness is driving the words we choose or the kind of advice that's given. Doctors may not have any idea they are doing this. When they offer yet another experimental drug, they may genuinely believe they know what's best for the patient. But *best*: Best is subjective. Best is your point of view. Best is what *you* want.

Being able to make a decision like this for another requires an understanding of each other, and time for self-reflection. You have to consider the painful, scary, and unwanted fact of separation. You are the proxy for the person in the bed. What she wants is all that counts. You want the person to live. Or you want the person to die your version of a "good" death. Or you want him to live another week until the rest of the family arrives. You want the gasping holler of pain in your chest to go away. Can you choose a course of treatment that will allow the person you love most

in the world to die? Can you say *no* on their behalf to something
you would choose for yourself? Can you say *yes* on their behalf
to an end you would never want? Can you set your own beliefs
to the side? This inevitable conflict of interest—you are dying
and I want you to live—is why a spouse or close family member
often should *not* be the one making all the decisions. You have to
ignore the begging chorus in your head, because it's not about
what *you* want.

In an old Japanese tradition, a person writes a poem on New Year's
Eve that will be read at their funeral if they die in the coming year.
A modern addition to this practice includes having a professional funeral photograph taken and picking out the clothing you want to
wear, in styles specially made for corpses. The Japanese word *jōjū*
means ever-present or unchanging. I like the translation "everlasting." The image of *jōjū* is often the moon. How can the moon, which
is never the same from night to night, be everlasting? And yet it is
always the same moon. *Jōjū* is that quality of unstoppable change and
the eternal at once. Death comes even while we are alive.

In the early 1700s, Mizuta Masahide, an admirer of the great
Bashō and a doctor by profession, had a fire at his home. It burned
down his storehouse, leaving his family impoverished. His poem
that year:

My storehouse burned down.
Now nothing stands between me
And the moon above.

Everlasting.

*   *   *

A dying person's attention turns toward a place we do not see and that they cannot explain. They are done with the business of the living, as it were, and more or less finished with us. Now they are not a mother or a plumber or a friend. Now they are entirely a dying person, and the world begins to shine. In spite of going hours without speaking, in spite of needing help to button a shirt, he is busy. He may not have the energy to talk, because he is waiting for something and that takes everything he has left.

He may be waiting to understand *why*.

Laugh. Laugh! Sing. The last kiss, the last dream, the last joke to tell. I have been telling you all the many things we might say, and shouldn't. Things to say as the end is coming: *I love you. I hope the best for you. We will be all right. Go with peace.*

Then we are listening again. We are returning to stillness, and to hearing what is being said without words. Most of us are not used to silence. It takes getting used to. The background noise of our lives is near-constant: endless voices, television, music, traffic, the ping from incoming texts, the demanding requests of daily life. Because we aren't used to silence, we don't understand how to be in it, how full it is. We may struggle against it, but silence is part of this world now. Silence is attention. Attention on this, right here, right now. Attention on the hand against the sheet, the texture of the cotton, the cool cotton. The hand rising to take a cup; the hard, warm curve of the cup. The steam. The heat. The sensation of the bending tendon in the hand, the scratch of a nail along the bedcover. Inhalation. Exhalation. All this in silence, filled with the music between words, what you might call the music of the spheres—the world's hum. The faint vibration of breath and muscle and time.

The writer Dennis Potter died of pancreatic cancer. A few months before his death, he gave a remarkable interview on the BBC. His wife was also dying, of breast cancer, and he was her main caregiver. He was relaxed and smiling—his pain cocktail was a combination of morphine, champagne, and cigarettes—and full of his signature dark humor. Dying, he said, gave him a new perspective on life; it gave him a way to celebrate.

"The blossom is out in full now," he said, describing what he saw from his office window. "It's a plum tree, it looks like apple blossom but it's white, and looking at it, instead of saying, 'Oh, that's a nice blossom' . . . last week looking at it through the window when I'm writing, I *see* it is the whitest, frothiest, blossomiest blossom that there ever could be, and I can see it. Things are both more trivial than they ever were, and more important than they ever were, and the difference between the trivial and the important doesn't seem to matter. But the nowness of everything is absolutely wondrous." He couldn't really explain, he added; you have to experience it. "The glory of it, if you like, the comfort of it, the reassurance . . . not that I'm interested in reassuring people, bugger that. The fact is, if you see the present tense, boy do you see it! And boy can you celebrate it."

He died nine days after his wife.

8

Last Days

Not long after Butch settled into his hospital bed in our living room, he began to slide away. His sobriety had been important to him. He'd been reluctant to use narcotics, but he eventually took small doses of morphine. He could not control his bladder or bowels. He didn't want to eat. This man who had spent most of his life in a struggle for safety and love had a ceaseless stream of affectionate visitors. He slept or lay quietly in bed most of the time. Now and then he would smile at the faces all around him. Cleo was there, and he knew he was in a safe place, and finally his pain was gone. He seemed to relax in a way I'd never seen in the five years I'd known him.

I helped him to the commode one mild, sunny afternoon. He was thin skin stretched across bones, closed eyes, fingers like spindles. As I helped him to lie down again, I said, "Butch, how do you feel?" And he made a sublime smile without opening his eyes. "Fantastic!" he said.

He never spoke again. Several hours later, in the middle of the night while we sat beside him, his breathing began to slow, and slow, and then it stopped.

To sit in vigil by a deathbed is a very old custom. It is usually a shared task. There may be prescriptions for who comes, and when, and what role they play, even where they sit in the room. In most of our history, death has been a social event, and still is in many places: a public occasion, because it affects everyone. Births and deaths bring the crowds, and the crowds seem to say, *This is what counts.*

Dying people can be quite clear about their needs, but they may also be opaque and symbolic. Either way, this is communication: needs, wants, wishes, regrets and fears, dreams and hope. Maggie Callanan and Patricia Kelley are experienced hospice nurses. In their book, *Final Gifts*, they describe many of the metaphorical and shadowed ways they have seen dying people communicate. They suggest keeping a notebook for everyone at the bedside to use, where they can write down what they hear and see, to help crack the code. They advise caregivers to "remember that there may be important messages in *any* communication, however vague or garbled." We who are watching may not know the value of a certain act, its past meaning or importance. A person may want to hold a necklace or look at a photograph that seems meaningless to you. You have no way of knowing what the meaning is, and may never know. If a dying person wants to hold a stuffed rabbit, find a stuffed rabbit. Find it quickly.

A dying person may rely on the vocabulary of the work they did, their family of origin, or their religion. Don't assume a person is confused just because he is responding to something that you don't see. He is telling you something. If he suddenly wants to get out of bed after being unable to stand, ask: *Are you leaving? Is it time to go?* Metaphors of travel are so common: packing luggage, buying a ticket, catching the ferry, wondering where the passport is, driving—and driving home. If a person says to you, *I want to go home now,* you may think to reassure them by saying, *You are already home.* But that may not be the home they mean. Perhaps they are thinking of their childhood home. They may mean the afterlife. A better answer might be: *It's okay to go home.*

Once a dying person has said goodbye, they are done saying goodbye. Listen to the farewell; say your own; say it once. Resist the urge to repeat yourself. You can't fairly ask a dying person to satisfy your emotional needs. Don't ask for forgiveness. (A person may ask for, or offer, forgiveness for an act no one else recalls.) Resist the urge to bring up "unfinished business," to seek "closure." Such things are due the dying alone, and many people do want to finish unfinished business, make amends, explain themselves. You are the witness; it's not yours to open that conversation. Your burden is yours to carry; don't ask a dying person to carry it for you.

I like to read obituaries, the miniature life stories filled with surprising details where one least expects surprise. One thing I notice—because I still have a little anxiety; I admit it—when I scan the list, is that almost everyone dies at an old age. Contrary to what our television watching habit may lead us to believe, most of us don't die at the hands of serial killers or from cancers that allow us to remain attractive or the malfeasance of a drunk driver. Most of us die as old or older than most people who have ever lived.

A few of my clients are in nursing homes. It will happen that I check in at the nurse's station and let the charge nurse know I'm there and who I've come to see, and I pat the desk and turn down the hall and find the room and knock and come in and find that the person I've come to see is taking his last uneven breath, without any warning. What do people die *of*, exactly? I used to visit a 105-year-old woman who lived in an assisted-living facility, in her own apartment with a kitchenette and bathroom, and a dining room down the hall. She was weak, but she could walk. She was terribly hard of hearing and watched daytime television with the volume full up. She had a tendency to adjust her underwear in the hallway, and a few other eccentric behaviors that are the rightful province of the very old. But she probably wouldn't have been eligible for hospice care, if she'd been interested.

An aide was helping her one day and left for a quarter of an hour to get linens. When she returned, the woman was dead. She had not been *dying*, exactly. She was just well past that supposedly divine term allowed to human beings, and died more or less exactly as I expected her to die: all at once, quietly, and alone.

The *Daily Telegraph* is famous for its death announcements: brief, laconic paragraphs, page after page of them. What strikes me is the picture of ease. Death seems simple, natural, expected. The brief announcements note that a person *died peacefully*, he was *much loved* or died *after a short illness and wonderful life of 93 years*; she was *surrounded by family*; she was *at her home*; he *died at 94 with his daughter by his side*. She *died suddenly at home, died suddenly but painlessly, passed away peacefully*. Over and over, every day. He was *very much loved*. She *died peacefully aged 99 of "old age."*

No one officially dies of old age. We die because something in the body fails, and in legal terms that's pathology, disease, injury. William Osler, the great nineteenth-century pulmonologist, called pneumonia "the friend of the aged." These days, we call it "the old man's friend." Pneumonia is one of the most common immediate causes of death in the world; it is quick and often seems painless. Death certificates list both the immediate and underlying causes of death, which may be pneumonia complicated by heart disease, or heart disease complicated by emphysema. (In other

words, old age.) There is good, civic sense in this. Death certificates tell us the history of our health as a group, which diseases
are common in different populations, which groups are at risk
for certain kinds of illness. Death certificates frame the inequi-
ties in health care. Without them, we wouldn't necessarily know
that African-American men die more frequently of cancer than
any other racial group, or that lung cancer rates are increasing
in middle-aged women. But they don't tell us that most of us die
from entropy.

The comedian Laurie Kilmartin used Twitter to describe her father's last days. Her comments were often funny and poignant:
"Just promised Dad I'd be nice to Mom. Damnit." She noted how
hard it was to be appropriate, to say the right thing. "Hospice says
to reassure the loved one that they can go, that we will be ok. So
me sobbing 'Dad, don't fucking leave me!' was frowned upon."

Yes, Laurie, you're right. Don't do that. Don't ask a person not
to die. (On the contrary. I saw a gerontologist I know stand by the
bedside of an old woman and say with a cheerleader's enthusiasm,
"C'mon, Margaret. You can do it!")

A group called No One Dies Alone provides volunteer companions for dying people who don't have visitors. I've always had
a little resistance to this—not that people should be left lonely in
their final months and weeks, but that our actual death has to have
an audience. We all die alone, and—more to the point—many
people will only die alone. People who haven't been left alone
for weeks will suddenly die in the one moment a caregiver or
spouse goes to the bathroom. Why? They may be trying to spare
a loved person; dying people can be just as polite, generous, and

modest as people who are in good health—and just as stubborn or profane or shy. A person may wait until the person they love most has enough help. And I'm not kidding about modesty. I cannot imagine a more intimate experience than the moment of my death, and I flinch a little at the vision of the Victorian parlor filled with neighbors and servants bearing chafing dishes. From where I stand today, I think I will want to share it with people close to me, will want to have a few hands to hold. But I don't know: perhaps the time will come and I will feel a powerful need to be alone in that solitary, unrepeatable experience.

So, be sure to give the person solitude for short periods, even if you're just in the next room. Announce it: *I'm going out for a few minutes.* It may not even be enough to say, *It's okay to go now. Don't worry about me.* You may need to be quite explicit: *It's fine to die now.*

My mother was in the hospital for the last several days of her life. She could no longer stand and really needed nurses around the clock. It was our small-town hospital, the place where my siblings and I had been born. My parents were both schoolteachers, and had taught some of the people who cared for her. The nurses quietly came in to do personal care, and otherwise left the family alone.

My father struggled. He was a reticent man and awkward with affection. He couldn't bear it. He'd seen the train coming for two years, and he couldn't bear it. "Pat," he cried, holding her hand. "Don't die. Don't go." She was unconscious, but he said this again and again. "Don't die. You haven't told me what color to paint the bedroom. Don't go. You can't die."

Knowing my father, I didn't expect anything else. I don't think he could have said that he loved her any other way, that he didn't know what to do, that he was shattered by her leaving. But I knew my mother, too. Finally, my sister in law, who was also a nurse, and I shooed everyone away. We said it was so we could turn her on her side, but it was really to get my father out of the room. Everyone else left, and we stood beside the bed silently. She took a single deep breath, and died.

A person approaching death from illness or age often changes in predictable ways. I believe that a lot of what a good nurse does at the end of life is looking. Looking and reminding: *Yes, this is normal. This is what happens. This is how we die. This is what it's like.* Everything is driven now by the person's comfort. Everything. Do check the temperature if you're worried about fever, because fever can be uncomfortable. Just check it under the arm. Pacemaker firing and causing discomfort? You can have it turned off. Stop the oxygen if it's bothering the person—and you will know it is because they will tug and pull at the tubing and take it off themselves as soon as you've turned your back. Comfort leads the way.

If a person becomes suddenly agitated or confused, be sure that an acute problem, such as an infection, is not being missed. Delirium is common and often can be treated. But health care providers do not always use terms like *confusion*, *delirium*, and *agitation* in consistent ways.

People who are dying get confused. How can they not? So much is happening: medication schedules and doctor appointments and visitors and bills and fatigue and lack of sleep. So much is happening so fast and at the same time that one's capacity is shrinking. Confusion is not delirium. Forgetting details, not following a conversation, missing an appointment—this is not delirium. If you are the helper, write it down. Whatever important details you say, write them down. Many caregivers will pin a note with details to the dying person's shirt; a note on your shirt tends to be found.

Delirium can be caused by many, many things: medication, low oxygen levels, anemia, kidney failure, changes in electrolyte levels, dehydration, pain or fever. In general, delirium comes on suddenly, in a few hours or days. (Dementia, by contrast, develops over months or years.) Seemingly all at once, the person is disoriented. He doesn't know where he is, who you are, what time it is, what year it is. He may be absolutely sure he is somewhere else. Attention fluctuates, waxing and waning. The person seems unable to remember what they are told and may speak in complex images or repetitive phrases or not be able to find the words they seek. There are active deliriums, in which the person is trying to climb out of bed and fights reassurance, and there are hypoactive deliriums, in which the person is lethargic and may simply lie there picking at the bedclothes and not responding. The person may hallucinate, not only visually but with tactile sensations, smells, and sounds. People often do remember what happens during a delirious state later and will say they could not control their perceptions or behavior.

Treatment starts with trying to fix the underlying problem. Meanwhile, reduce the stimulus in the room: Lower the lights, keep voices down. You might play familiar music quietly. Music pulls us into the past that has made us who we are, and into the body. Scents can be calming. The most well-known is lavender, which acts on the central nervous system. What scents did the person choose when they were able? Is their bedroom lined with scented candles? Did the person wear perfume or a particular aftershave? A really excited delirious person may need sedating medications just for safety, but the doctor should be very cautious about this so as not to make things worse.

Terminal agitation is a sudden outburst of energy and excitement that happens in the last days or hours of life. People may shout and try to climb out of bed or strike out at caregivers, talk and laugh and cry, or simply roll from side to side. The restlessness can be dramatic and distressing: Grandma gets up on her hands and knees and starts shouting. First, rule out a physical cause, especially pain. People who work with the dying are familiar with this state, and it often does not seem to have a physical cause but rather to be a kind of blunt expression of emotion. And why are we surprised by strong emotion or wild energy at such a time?

A woman who cared for her mother when she was dying of liver cancer described the many episodes of excitement and agitated movement in her mother's last few days. "Her moments of agitation seemed to me to resemble contractions during child-birth, or the stations of the cross, a kind of labour. The labour of letting go."

Reorientation doesn't usually work. You may ask questions (*Who do you see? What are you doing?*). Freely offer forgiveness and reassurance even if none seems necessary. If a person seems distressed, say, *I love you, you are safe, don't be afraid.* (Take a few moments to consider if the distress is yours alone.) If nothing else works, physical causes (other than dying) are ruled out, and the agitation seems distressing to the person, there are medications. Lorazepam is common, and Haldol may be used. People sometimes fear this drug, but it is a well-known and easily managed medication that can dramatically help when a person is unable to control themselves.

The opposite happens, too. Many people—and this is one of

those anecdotal truths, a story everyone who works in this field knows—perk up just before they die. This is sometimes described as "terminal lucidity." Terminal lucidity is well documented, happens to people of all ages, all different kinds of illness and intellectual status, even in dementia, even with brain tumors, even in people who have not spoken in years. A person who has been mostly asleep or withdrawn will suddenly be more alert, oriented, and may even start talking. It is easy to imagine that the last of the resistance is gone. The simplest explanation may be that she knows it's time.

These last days, last hours, are filled with change. Certain behaviors that may look like pain—agitation, for instance—may not be pain. But, yes, there is pain sometimes, and a few people struggle for good pain control. Believe what a person says. If a person isn't speaking, watch for nonverbal signs like grimacing or a tight facial expression, tight or contracted muscles or posture, rapid breathing. Pain raises blood pressure and heart rate in most people. Try to console or distract a person who seems to be in pain; inconsolability is a sign of significant pain.

A person may need more pain medication toward the end of life, but many people need less. Remember not to stop or change any drug abruptly without checking with the doctor or nurse. Morphine can suppress the depth of breathing as well as the rate, so it is given cautiously in people with respiratory issues. If a person is very close to death and takes a high enough dose of morphine, it is possible for the breathing to be suppressed. The Supreme Court has ruled more than once on what is called the "doctrine of double effect." If the intention is relief of suffering, then the possibility of hastening an inevitable death cannot be prosecuted as a crime. Whether or not morphine actually hastens a particular death, it is possible; the goal is not an extra hour of life but a painless death.

Suffering is a deeply felt threat to the integrity of the self. It means that we hold on to the hope that something will remain unchanged even as it all slides away like sand in running water, like water from our hands. We can have physical pain and not suffer; we can suffer without physical pain. A very few people may have uncontrollable pain. A few other symptoms of dying can become intractable—unmanageable with drugs and nursing care. Severe dyspnea, delirium, uncontrolled nausea, muscle spasms, and depression are rare but do occur.

There are other forms of suffering: psychological, emotional, and spiritual suffering are all recognized. People can get stuck trying to die. Callanan and Kelley call this "being held back," an aspect of being aware of nearing death. A person who has been restful suddenly becomes upset. Do they need to see a particular person or write a private letter? Or confess? "Telling us about 'being held back' is a way dying people have of asking us to 'look again: something's been missed!'" There is a person they need to see, a goodbye to be said, plans that must be made, paperwork to sign. An anniversary to reach. Shame to be reconciled. A crime to be punished. Love to be returned. The things may seem long gone or unimportant to you, but they are filling the world of the dying person. Don't diminish or dismiss such concerns.

A person who feels terror at God's coming judgment or a sense of irrevocable sin is in spiritual distress. In early European Christianity, a person who died while in the process of conversion would be buried with their head inside the sacred ground and their feet outside. A person who feels they have not been wholly forgiven by God or the Church is likely to feel great distress; he is disconnected from any sense of wholeness, powerless, and without peace.

Existential pain comes to all of us, is woven into the fact of being human. But existential distress is a crisis. This is sometimes called "unbearable suffering," a legal concept. People can feel panic about death, experience great hopelessness and despair or awful remorse. They may have no sense of self-worth, or they may be terrified of dependence and the loss of control. A person may simply feel very scared about the experience of death itself. They are not clinically depressed or delirious. They are just suffering in a particularly terrible way: facing what cannot be stopped without any composure.

If a person is suffering from physical problems or deep existential distress is high, he can be treated with what is called palliative sedation. This essentially means letting a person sleep their way to death. Strict criteria are applied. This is a treatment of last resort, used when all other treatments—psychotherapy, drugs, meditation, nursing care, pastoral help, hypnosis—have failed. Usually a DNR order must be in place and informed consent obtained. No futile treatments, such as tube feedings, can be used.

Respite sedation is tried first: a period of one to two days of sleep brought on by strong medications like Thorazine, Haldol, and Versed. Midazolam has the quality of inducing amnesia for the period of time it is used. Respite sedation can allow a person exhausted from fear to rest, "thereby," in the words of one researcher, "allowing patients the opportunity to regain psychological strength in order to face the existential issues that precipitated the sedation." In other words, sedation may be a break from the overwhelming experience of dying, so that a person becomes strong enough to face dying again.

I describe this, not because you or anyone you love is likely to need it, but because you may be afraid that you or someone you love will suffer. You will not have to suffer.

And, yes, here we are along this line, this veiled time when none of us sees entirely clearly, here at the very end of life where a lot of things begin to blur. Where we talk about double effect and also about assisted death. Where we see the joy of nowness and palliative sedation. Where we are forced to confront the fact that we have ideals, that we believe things should go a certain way, and that certain things should be said and done. Where we discover that a prognosis can be wrong, goodbyes are not always said, and death can be messy. Where we find out that we do believe only a certain kind of death is a good death.

In Jewish law, a person at the edge of death who is expected to die within three days is a particular kind of creature, a *goses*—a person between life and death. The word is said to come from the sound of the breath in the last hours of life. In Jewish tradition, such a person should not be touched or disturbed except as necessary to provide medical and nursing care, in case such touching might hasten the death. Any required touch should be as gentle as possible. The room is kept quiet and serene, with talking limited to loving reassurance. Visitors leave to eat or drink or have conversations but are careful not to leave the dying person alone lest they feel abandoned.

No one is really alone at the moment of death, perhaps, because the membrane is very thin here: between past and present, life and death, corporeal and ephemeral, body and mind. Dying people sometimes appear to have spiritual experiences; these are known as "deathbed phenomena." People gesture and wave, seem to hold invisible objects, or arrange items or mime doing something like cooking or knitting. Perhaps it is biochemistry, or memory, or dream. We cannot know. A person who has never done so before may begin to pray or sing religious songs. In various large studies—involving thousands of people—as many as half of the families interviewed said their dying relative appeared to talk to people who were not there, have visions, or describe visiting other worlds or seeing bright lights. A woman may appear to hold and cradle a baby; men will reach to hug an invisible person. Mysteries. A dying person will occasionally predict the day or time of their death. And notice the expression on the person's face. Is she happy? Is she, finally, at peace? A woman listened to her dying husband have a long conversation with the corner of the room, as though someone were standing there. When she asked him what was going on, he said, "I can't talk to you now, I'm busy. I'll talk with you in the morning." The next day he told her that people were helping him get ready: "Surely you must know that I'm living in two worlds now." Later she found him sitting on the edge of the bed, gesturing as though he were eating a grand meal. "We're having a party," he explained. Callanan and Kelley note: "The most important thing to remember when a dying person sees someone invisible to you is that death is not lonely."

Don't dismiss such experiences, try to explain or define, or—oh, please don't—"reorient" the person to the fact that they are imagining something. Instead, listen to what is said. Watch. Ask questions. Be patient. Most people who have witnessed this feel the experiences were deeply comforting and important, and brought peace to the dying person.

If you're at the bedside, provide safety. The reaching, picking, and gesturing, the conversations and parties, can become an urgent need to get up, climb out of bed, and go. Protect the person from an accidental fall.

The rest is mystery. I like to think the person is wayfinding; they are holding a kind of compass in their hands, looking for the path. I think of the lovely song by Rickie Lee Jones called "Running from Mercy," a song high on my own playlist for dying. In her inimitable murmur, she sings, "There's that door / I've got that door / I know where that door is."

Fantastic. Most people stop speaking days or even weeks (or years) before death, and no one can remember their last words. But some people remain conscious until the last hours of life— even to the final minute—and these last words can be wonderful. Cotton Mather, an ambiguous role model if there ever was one and not a man known for exaltation, is reported to have said, "Is this dying? Is this all? Is this all that I feared, when I prayed against a hard death? O! I can bear this! I can bear it! I can bear it!" When Anton Chekhov was very ill, he left Russia for a spa in Germany. One day he sent for the doctor. When he arrived, Chekhov said simply, "I am dying." The doctor's answer is not recorded. Champagne was considered a good medicine for heart conditions at the time, and Chekhov was persuaded to take a few sips. He hadn't, he quietly remarked, had champagne in ages. *I haven't had champagne in ages.* Then he closed his eyes and died. (His body was sent back to Russia in a refrigerated train car, in a box labeled "Oysters.")

I don't think it matters if we are conscious or unconscious when we die; the line between awake and asleep is a little like the other arbitrary boundaries we draw. Most people aren't awake, but what kind of consciousness they have remains a mystery. Lots of people say they want to die in their sleep. They don't want to deal with the dying part at all. Marge Piercy: "I want to click the off switch." I do want to be awake; that's the curious part of me, not wanting to miss a minute of life but also not wanting to miss any of this singular, unrepeatable event. What is more likely is that I will fall into this peculiar sleep like no other. I don't know what kind of dream I will have.

Doctors and nurses use the phrase *active dying* to indicate the last few days or hours of life when certain marked physical changes can be seen. We forget the oddity of this phrase. People wonder if it means death is happening right now, this minute. Does it hurt? And how can you *actively* die if you're lying there unconscious? But dying is not a passive event. We can't control it, but we do participate in it. We aren't simply watching or waiting for *something* to happen *to* us. We are *dying*, and this is a verb. An act.

A familiar complex of signs tells us death is very close. People who are close to dying become profoundly weak and eventually can no longer move at all. The anal sphincter loosens, and bowel control is lost. The person is incontinent; he may have difficulty urinating. In time, he stops making urine; the kidneys fail and so urine production slows, the urine becomes dark and concentrated, and then stops. Near death, as the kidneys shut down and circulation begins to collapse, the pH of the blood changes. The ratio of electrolytes that control muscles and nerves change, too, and sometimes people have jerking limbs, tremors and heaves, or itching. The hands and feet may become cool and mottled. Arms and legs will swell as circulation begins to fail. A dying body withdraws to the center: oxygen and energy are directed inward, as if in shock; mind, awareness, turned in. As death approaches, the sensorium becomes clouded—seeing, hearing, smell and taste, tactile sensations, all dull. Eyes glaze over or stay half-open; a person may stop blinking. Brain-stem auditory evoked responses (BAERs) that measure hearing are normal in comatose people. Many people who have awakened from comas remember conversations that took place in the room. Always assume people can hear you. Thermal regulation breaks down. People may have terminal fever and sweat copiously. The skin may be hot and dry, hot and damp, cold and damp. They may have hiccups.

Breathing speeds up, slows down, becomes uneven. Sometimes breaths are very deep, or a breath is skipped. Breathing may completely stop for several seconds, which is called apnea. The rate and depth of breathing may vary in either a regular or unpredictable way. Cheyne-Stokes respiration is variable but somewhat regular: apnea, shallow breaths, deep, hyperventilating breaths, shallow breaths, apnea. Biot's respiration, which I actually see more often than Cheyne-Stokes, is an unpredictable variation of apnea with breathing of an irregular rhythm. The person may also grunt at times, or grunt with each exhalation or gasp. Sometimes a person will seem to use their shoulders almost like a bellows, up and down with every breath. A person may seem to chew with each breath, or the jaw sags and the mouth hangs open.

Apneustic breathing can be caused by brain damage, such as from a stroke or trauma: a rapid pattern of shallow breaths, with a long but shallow inhalation and weak, ineffective exhalations. At the very end of life, or in cardiac arrest, you may see agonal breaths, which are weak and gasping. Agonal breaths often have an odd noise. Apneustic and agonal breaths cannot sustain life; they are signs that death is very close. Notice the change. Consider leaving the room briefly in case they need to be alone. You might touch a person's feet or hands. It is perfectly all right to be silent. You might want to get in bed with the person and simply rest together. Be as present to this, right now, here, as you can. No need for words. *I know where the door is.*

One part of normal dying is particularly distressing to caregivers and family: a kind of noisy breathing commonly called the death rattle. Noisy breathing is a normal part of dying, very common. People often die within a day after it starts. We clear our throats frequently without thinking about it; noisy breathing happens when a person becomes too weak to clear their normal secretions. Breathing sounds moist and may have a quality of crackling or gurgling.

Medications may help a little by drying up secretions. But the drugs are only useful for about half of patients, and almost all patients have significant negative side effects. Is it worth quieting this sound at the cost of confusion, restlessness, dry mouth, and sedation? Nevertheless, such medications are often prescribed in what hospice staff call "treating the family." There is no reason to think a person is bothered by the rattle, because signs of discomfort aren't seen with noisy breathing. A woman who watched her father die remembered that his breathing sounded awful to those in the room; their distress was obvious. But he was alert. He saw the distress. In between his irregular, failing breaths, in his last minutes—in what had to be a final act of parental generosity—he gasped out the words, "No pain."

Caregivers can help reduce some of the noise by turning a person on his side. Often one side is more comfortable than another. You can use firm pillows under a person's shoulders and behind the back and legs to help keep the person in this position. It may be helpful to roll a person from one side to the other every few hours. But remember that noisy and uneven breathing is a natural part of dying. Think about whether you are treating your own discomfort.

When organs are beginning to fail, a spiral begins in which toxins accumulate and cells are deprived of oxygen. Sherwin Nuland described actual death as "a process in which every tissue of the body partakes, each by its own means and at its own pace. The operative word here is *process*, not *act*, *moment*, or any other term connoting a flyspeck of time when the spirit departs." The body, that magnificent, complex, beloved system of systems, is failing. As each part fails a little, the homeostasis of the entire system begins to fail. Each system tumbles gently into the next like dominoes. The heart rate and respirations may speed up, or slow down, or just change for no apparent reason. By-products of metabolism break down in acidosis, and the room may suddenly smell sweet.

The great thirteenth-century Zen master known as Dōgen died in his fifties—something of a ripe age at the time. During his last illness, he wrote a poem about going to Yellow Springs, the Shinto land of the dead:

> *For fifty-four years*
> *Sinning against heaven;*
> *Now leaping beyond,*
> *Hah! To cast off all attachments,*
> *Living, I leap into the Yellow Springs.*

Alive, he leaps. Can I be curious about that leap? Heart pounding, palms damp, but curious? About what happens next? Can I be interested in this moment, which is unlike any other? Can I leap into the unknown springs, knowing there is no other choice, with arms open wide?

When I watch snow falling, I see the transformation of the world into a smooth plane where differences disappear. The snow falls in fragments so delicate that a mere breath can destroy them—the way moments fall, the way our life passes by. It covers the earth with something strong and solid and pure. Each of us may be nothing more than a moving wave of change, but we are waves able to know that. We rise and fall in an infinitely deep and timeless sea, upright and undisturbed. This is the other side of our dangerous situation. Dying is perfectly safe. It isn't going to hurt you.

9

That Moment

Such wonder. With my eyes closed, I can tell. When the Buddha died, Ananda, one of his most devout attendants, said, "My hair stood up." Do we have a constant, subconscious awareness of the pulse, a microscopic attention to the flow of blood? Do we know life as something electrical? Pheromonal? Ethereal? The follicles on the back of your neck salute in surprise. For the first time since conception, the body is still. *Stopped.* Life is tension, life is animation, movement, tone, elasticity. Not this.

At the moment of death, a thousand tiny things happen. A fading, a flattening out. The eyes become cloudy and appear to sink. The face turns flaccid and the jaw sags. The skin falls into shapes never seen in life. The face with which you are so familiar, upon which you have gazed so many times, is that of a stranger. A mask. A dead body is like nothing else in the world: a carcass, hollow, an object lesson in Newton's law—we are bodies in motion, staying in motion. A corpse is a body at rest. We call it a body in repose, and rarely use this word in other contexts. It is from the Middle English; the original meaning is to replace, to put back. Maurice Merleau-Ponty believed that we give meaning to objects by using them. The meaning of the self is in its function. He called this

intentionality, and death a kind of "slackening" in the wires of intention. To look at a corpse a moment after death is to see in the
most incontrovertible way that we are creatures of intent.

Take your time. There is no hurry at all. No hurry, no need
to move a body quickly or cover it up or leave the room. Look.
Please, do look. Something profound has happened in this room.
It may have been noisy and may have been silent. You may be
calm; you may be distraught. No matter. Take your time.

And yet death is not a single moment at all—or, rather, it is a very
long moment, defined in different ways. Anticipated after a long
illness, death is a breath, then no breath for a few seconds, for
many seconds. Then another breath. A loud gasp. Then breathing
again. Then no breath. I have seen people breathe four times a
minute, three times a minute. Once a minute. One breath, half a
breath, the respiratory center's last command. There is scant but
intriguing evidence that delta waves in the brain continue for a
few minutes after this. Even moments after death, miniscule electrical signals can fire—the tiniest twitch of an eyelid or lip.

Which breath is the last one?

This is our conventional wisdom: that a person is dead when
the heartbeat ends and breathing stops. We agree that the time of
death for a person on a ventilator is when the machine is turned
off and the heart stops—but sometimes we turn the machine off
because we believe the brain is dead and there is no *person* left at
all. The body is designed to preserve itself, to continue. When
this work stops in such a way that it can't be started again, when
the drive to live—most succinctly framed as a reflexive need
to breathe—is gone, we may say a person is dead. The body's

organization as a system of systems is lost. Do we die with the
last breath, or the last heartbeat, or the last brain wave? Yes. No.
Maybe. Choose. Time of death is as much a social agreement as
a clinical one. In Japan, people disagree about how and when a
person dies. By law, the patient who is anticipating her death, or a
family member making decisions for the patient, can declare their
preference for which definition of death will prevail.

We think of life and death as opposites: opposed to each other,
two sides in a battle. They cancel each other out. Perhaps life and
death are entirely separate and whole events taking place without
regard for the other.

We die each moment, become new selves each moment. When
I am afraid, I know it is this bounded self that fears, the aggregates
of body and mind bound together. This irreplaceable self. The
insights I've had into the heaving sea of change are like the iris of
the eye snapping open all the way for an instant. Such insights give
us a glimpse of how things fit together. What I've experienced in
such moments is so similar to experiences described by people
of different religions or no religious faith at all that it would be
foolish to claim them for a belief system. The words we choose
are like coloring, like the scribbles of crayons on the surface of a
sphere; it is the sphere with which we are concerned. As we approach the moment of death, all our underlying beliefs are starkly
outlined. Our sense of what a human life encompasses—the room
a human being takes up in the world, and whether there is something greater or everlasting beyond human life—is framed in a
stark light. I stand now on a ground of fearlessness altogether different from the anxieties of my ambitious youth. The poet Marie
Howe imagines the moment of death not as an ending, the halting
of something, but as a point of completion. A totaling of a life.

The eternal memory of the tired satisfaction at the end of a good day, a satisfaction never before known: *At last / someone has knotted the lace of your shoe so it won't ever come undone.* I am not who I was fifty years ago, or ten years ago, or last year, or yesterday. I am not the person who wrote this sentence. Which of me will die? This moment in which everything, everything, everything changes at once is one of great mystery, great power, like no other moment in all of time.

10

Bodies

A person is not just a body; a person has a body," writes the philosopher Daniel Dennett. "That corpse is the body of dear old Jones, a Center of Narrative Gravity." Why does it matter what we do with a body, knowing that the person no longer exists? Or doesn't exist in the sense of proximal intentionality—so why would the body have meaning? Yet it does, it always does; whether we cling to it or flee it, what happens to the emptied body feels momentous. As long as we will continue to live, we will remember what happened to the body of the one who died. Dennett thinks we have to care for dead bodies, because to do otherwise threatens the living. "The boundaries of Jones are not identical to the boundaries of Jones's body," he writes. Jones is not here anymore; in a relationship, we are in a kind of ceaseless conversation with each other, and that conversation is done. But the corpse is still part of the story, even if it isn't part of the telling. "If we start treating corpses as garbage, for instance," writes Dennett, "it might change the way we treat near-corpses—those who are still alive but dying." The corpse is a mirror; we are its reflection.

The range of attitudes toward the corpse are as varied as humankind, but whatever is done, it carries the weight of a ritual object. In many societies, the disposal of the body depends on the status of the dead person. Australian Aboriginal culture has a number of rules about how and when and by whom a corpse is touched. The dead one is given a death name, called a necronym. Cannibalism is considered a sign of respect in certain societies. On the island of Sulawesi, families keep the body of a dead relative for several years while it slowly mummifies. The body is dressed, given a plate of food at the table, perhaps a cigar or glass of liquor now and then. Even after the mummy is entombed, the coffins are sometimes opened so the clothes can be changed. We can eat the body in little candy skulls on the Day of the Dead, shouting and singing behind our masks, controlling death by digesting it. One culture brings flowers to the graves of loved ones and carves their names in stone; another culture avoids graves at all costs. One builds mausoleums for expensive coffins and another ceremoniously tosses the bodies off a cliff.

Even within a society, people make diametrically opposite choices about how to dispose of the dead. In the modern West, one family keeps the ashes on the mantel, next to the photographs; the other family cleans out the closets and paints the bedroom as soon as the funeral is over. One person applies to be a plastinated model, and another considers it a gross, irreligious display.

The "fuzzy" ambiguity right after death is expressed in many ways. In Shinto belief, a dead person is ambiguous: still human but unlike the living. He has become an infant again in important ways. Soon after death, a close relative touches the corpse's lips with a wet cloth, a double-edged symbol: the offering is a final effort to revive the person and, at the same time, proof that he is dead. In Jewish tradition, the eyes and mouth of the dead are closed and the body is covered with a sheet. The windows are opened, the mirrors are covered, and the body is never left unattended. Jewish funeral homes offer the services of a *shomer*, who watches over the body prior to the funeral. The *shomer* doesn't eat or drink in the presence of the corpse; such behavior is considered mocking, because the dead cannot do these things.

There is usually no need to hurry to move a body. Changes happen over hours and days, not minutes. American law generally allows you to leave a body in place for at least twenty-four hours. A hospital may give you much less time, but that's as much convention as anything else. Ask for more time. Tell the nurse you're not ready. They will charge you another night's rent eventually, but you don't *have* to go, especially if you have religious obligations. You don't have to do anything for a long time, and then you can do it your way. (The one thing you have to do is register the death according to the local laws.)

Rainer Maria Rilke wrote a poem called *Corpse Washing*: "And one without a name lay / there, bare and cleansed, and gave commands." Washing a body is an act of submission. We surrender to the fact of death. There is no need to do this, but bathing a body is an almost universal act, the instinctive response of grief, and it feels as though something is being done for all of us when we do.

Many Japanese die at home. The traditional Shinto way of caring for a dead body is called *nōkan*, or "encoffinment," practiced by artisans known as *nōkanshi*. In Japan, dead bodies were long considered impure, and this was a vital but low occupation. The *nōkanshi* prepares the body while the family watches. The entire corpse is wiped clean under draping, taking care for modesty and never exposing the body to view. Facial hair is shaved and then makeup applied, to both men and women. Done correctly, encoffinment has all the Japanese virtues of proportion and precise movement, coupled with the blunt fact of what lies before you. The clothes are folded with intention, the hands posed carefully, the facial expression arranged just so. At the end of the ritual, the body is carefully lifted and placed in the coffin. Younger people seem less concerned with impurity these days, and encoffinment has been somewhat rebelliously revived as a profession. There is a small *nōkanshi* competition at the annual Life Ending Industry Expo in Japan to see who can do this most beautifully.

Take your time. Washing a body is difficult to do alone, and why should we? Share the experience. A dead body, deflated, shrunken, feels somehow heavier than a living one. It is awkward to move. If you have ever felt the weight of a sleeping person, know that this weight isn't the same. Even a person sound asleep carries his own body with the tension of living muscle. A dead body has no tension at all; it is sand, water, stone.

Go slowly. Lay down towels or pads first, as the bladder and bowels may drain when the body is moved. This is the easiest way to move a dead body: two or more people on each side roll the sheet up tightly against the body and slide and lift together. Be prepared for the body to sigh or groan; when you turn a body, the last air is released from the lungs. Take your time, take a deep breath. Think it through. We know how to hold a baby, how to hold each other, and we know how to hold a body.

We are exquisitely tuned to the sensation of another's skin, to the texture and warmth of living skin. Skin is the largest organ in the body; when we touch each other, we are touching a vital organ. A corpse's skin will not feel like this. Under living skin is a continual humming pulse of moving blood and dividing cells, a vibration of electrical signals in the muscles, the shiver of nerve response. Dead skin is inelastic and fragile at once. A corpse may appear to sweat and feel clammy. The body temperature drops by almost two degrees Fahrenheit every hour after death, in a process called algor mortis.

The beloved lies before you, completely revealed. All of aging, every success and every injury, the ragged ending of illness or trauma, all of the lived life, is revealed: the farmer's tan lines; the sparse, unevenly shaved legs; the hysterectomy scar and pregnancy stretch marks; the callused heels and poorly cut toenails; arthritic knuckles and the roots of gray hair at the bottom of the dye. We spend our lives wishing our bodies were different than they are: younger, stronger, bigger, thinner, curvier, prettier, taller, *different*. The point comes when you find out what you already know about the people you love. Concealment is gone, disguise is yanked away, and so are all our efforts at disguise and our shallow desire to be disguised, our yearning to be seen as other than we are. Everything shows. Should we be surprised by what we see? This is time: the roughened, slumping body. When we see another exactly as he is, exactly as she is, we see how much alike we are. Love is really the only possible response. You need warm, wet cloths and love. Love is useful here.

Wash the body and dress it. The body may ooze fluid afterward, so if the clothing being put on is important, start with an incontinent pad or brief, or wrap a towel around the genitals. When you are done bathing and dressing, move the body into the desired position. Rigor mortis starts within a few hours after death, with chemical changes in the muscle cells. This happens more quickly in the cold, and if a person was working hard just before dying.

Rigor starts with involuntary muscles: the bowel, heart, bladder and other organs. Rigor then spreads to the head and neck, stiffening the jaw and eyelids, and then into the trunk and limbs. If the body has begun to stiffen, move the limbs with slow, steady pressure. If you want to cross the arms over the chest or put the hands together, you may need to bind them gently with cloth, or interlace the fingers. Roll a small towel under the neck to support the head. Place a clean cloth or gauze pad over the eyes. This can be gently taped in place or held down by a small bag of rice or other light weight. Dentures may be difficult to place or remove. If the lower jaw won't close, roll a washcloth into a tube and place it under the chin. You can also use a scarf, being careful to smooth out all wrinkles. Place the scarf on the head and wrap it gently around the chin and tie on top. Leave the scarf and eye bag in place for a few hours and the body will set in this posture.

You may want a photograph. In the small town where I grew up, we had two cemeteries: the big city cemetery where my relatives were buried, and a small traditional Catholic cemetery on a hill. My friends and I hiked up there now and then to look at the gravestones. Each had a pair of photographs, side-by-side images of the person alive and the person in a coffin, a practice I found spooky and exciting. (Recalling this, I think those photographs are the first real images of dead people that I ever saw.) Once, photos of the dead dressed and posed as though alive were prized. Many people still make death masks, or a model of a loved one's hands, or art from their hair, teeth, or fingernails. Now is the time to take a memento—a memento mori, the Latin for "Remember, you must die."

When Butch died, we cleaned him up and laid him straight. After everyone had taken their time to say goodbye—several hours, as I remember—we called the service and two men in black suits came in the soft afternoon sun. They slid him onto the stretcher and tucked a sheet around him and belted the body in tight. Then the older man asked, "Would he want sunshine on his face, or not?" And we all said at once, "Sunshine." They left his face exposed and carried him away, tilting the stretcher up on the outside steps so that he faced the sun one last time.

These were nice men, and I am glad for that memory. But you can take the body to a mortuary or crematorium by yourself. People have been known to dress a body and strap it into the passenger seat with a rakish hat on for the ride. How about a motorcycle sidecar? An important thing to know about disposing of a body is that you do not need to use a funeral home. You don't have to have a funeral. You do not need to use a hearse or a coffin. You can speak to cemeteries and crematoriums directly and prepare the body yourself. You don't need pallbearers, but the reason six strong men may be required is the coffin. Most bodies can be carried by four women. Biodegradable coffins are light and can be carried with straps, and many shrouds have handles for this purpose. In some cemeteries, you can dig the grave yourself.

As long as you are following local law, you can bury the body on your own land. This is often an entirely personal choice requiring no contact with authorities. (Local ordinances vary. A man in Stevenson, Alabama, buried his wife in his yard according to her wishes and has been fighting exhumation and reburial ever since. So far, she's still there.)

You don't have to do any of the things many people do with dead bodies, but hardly anyone is going to volunteer this information. The Natural Death Centre of the UK advises that if a funeral director tells you that you must do this or that, "you may want to consider choosing another funeral director."

Under English common law, no one owns a dead body and a dead body owns nothing: "The only lawful possessor of a corpse is the earth." Artists have sued to keep embalmed bodies and have both won and lost. Laws about the dead are ever-evolving and contradictory even now.

In 1905, Georgia Supreme Court justice Joseph Henry Lumpkin II ruled in a case in which a widow sought damages from a train company that had left her husband's coffin in the rain, resulting in "mutilation" of the corpse. An earlier case had held that the corpse, once buried, belonged to the ground; improperly digging it up would be merely trespass. But another case deemed a corpse "quasi-property," recognizing that kin have an interest in the corpse even though it belongs to no one. This concept is widely held today; it may be phrased as having the right to "take possession" of the body and dispose of it.

In the widow's case, Lumpkin wrote, "Death is unique. It is unlike aught else in its certainty and its incidents. A corpse in some respects is the strangest thing on earth. A man who but yesterday breathed and thought and walked among us has passed away. Something has gone. The body is left still and cold, and is all that is visible to mortal eye of the man we knew. Around it cling love and memory. Beyond it may reach hope. It must be laid away. And the law—that rule of action which touches all human things—must touch also this thing of death. It is not surprising that the law relating to this mystery of what death leaves behind cannot be precisely brought within the letter of all the rules regarding corn, lumber and pig iron." The court ruled in favor of the widow.

In France, a dead person can get married in certain circumstances, because a dead *person* may have rights of a certain kind. A dead *body* does not have rights, including the right to be buried as the once-living person had wished to be buried. Only a living person can make a wish. Even so, we should make our wishes known. The person who will decide what will happen to your body is your executor or personal representative. Be sure you choose one who will honor your wishes, and be sure you've told them what you want. Your body is the last object for which you can be responsible, and this wish may be the most personal one you ever make. It is an act of kindness not to leave this decision to bereft family members, who may fight among themselves, spend too much money, and collapse in pressured compromise. You have no need to apologize for what you want. Maybe you want to be coiffed and made up; maybe you want to be fed to vultures. Just save those who love you from trying to guess.

The funeral home (or "death care") industry has been moving toward economies of scale and massive multinational corporate ownership for decades. (I don't know exactly what this is telling us about the world, but a robotics team has designed a machine that can wash, dry, and even shroud a body automatically. They designed it in accordance with Islamic law, but are willing to change the plans to "conform to other religions / customs.")

The biggest funeral corporation by far is SCI (Service Corporation International, a deliberately meaningless name). SCI owns a huge fraction of the industry, including the brands National Cremation Service, Neptune Society, Dignity Memorial, and Advantage Funeral & Cremation Services. In the last few years, SCI bought its two largest competitors, Alderwoods Group and Stewart Enterprises. Annual revenues are in the billions of dollars, with more than two thousand funeral homes and cemeteries in forty-five US states, eight Canadian provinces, the District of Columbia, and Puerto Rico. (Buying Stewart Enterprises is forcing SCI to sell off some properties to comply with monopoly laws.) SCI sometimes buys family-run mortuaries in order to trade on respected names; nothing appears to change, not the name or even the staff. If you want to make sure a funeral home or crematorium is the independent local business it appears to be, you have to ask.

If you are not sure what to do with a dead body, don't start with a funeral home. Start with the Funeral Consumers Alliance, a national organization with clear, concise information and suggestions intended to help people get what they want at a fair price. In an interview, Joshua Slocum, the executive director, said, "If we treated car buying the way we treated funeral buying, we would walk into the Honda dealer and hold our hands out and say to the first salesman on the floor, 'Um, I need a car. What do I need, and how much will it cost?' But this is exactly how we buy funerals." Instead, he suggests, we should put on "our grown-up pants" and be good consumers.

By the time my mother died, she'd had breast cancer for two years, a double radical mastectomy, a broken hip, and liver failure. She was yellowed, gaunt, with swollen limbs, her hair thinned to transparency. The day after she died, I took my father to the funeral home to pick out a casket. My father was a firefighter and wouldn't consider cremation. The funeral director happened to be one of my parents' best friends. He sold my father the most expensive coffin available and assured him that it would be waterproof.

Two days later, we returned for the viewing. We were led into the "Slumber Room," but after a few steps, I stopped in shock. For

one weird moment in that strange marginal land of acute grief—
for one long and very eerie moment—I thought my mother
was alive again. She looked better than she had for years, almost
plump, her skin glowing and warm, her hair full. Even her nails
were done. I found it difficult to go closer. I had the irrational
thought, and I knew it was irrational and illogical, and I couldn't
shake it, that she might sit up. I didn't want that. I didn't want this
false life.

To this day, I resent what was done to my mother. (To me.) I
had attended deaths, washed bodies, done cadaver dissection. But
hers was the first body that spooked me. I was just thirty years
old; I wanted her to live—we all longed for her to live—but she
died. I had seen it coming; I had come to believe it, to accept it.
But when I saw her in the funeral home looking as though she
might turn and smile at me, a lot of my hard-won acceptance was
knocked loose. The next day the lid was sealed on her heavy waterproof metal casket, and she was buried.

Embalming was considered strange in the United States until
the twentieth century. In the Civil War, great numbers of people
died away from home, and thousands of officers were experi-
mentally embalmed. (Lincoln himself was famously embalmed to
allow the long public mourning his death invoked.) But the odd
practice didn't catch on. The growing size of the country meant
that funerals sometimes had to be delayed. Bodies that couldn't be
buried quickly were packed in ice, and occasionally suspended in
alcohol. Neither method was entirely reliable, and the occasional
failure was spectacular.

Embalming is still uncommon in Europe. In many parts of the
world, it is so unusual that a special permit is required to do so.
But over a very short period, starting in the 1930s, embalming be-

came normal in the United States. By the early twentieth century, American society had changed. People were dying more often in hospitals than at home, and homes were smaller and closer together while families were more scattered and wandering. Religion had lost a little of its hold on daily life. The profession of "undertaker"—a professional who could handle all the complex details of a funeral—appeared. Embalming allowed for more time.

Jewish law generally forbids embalming, for reasons I find familiar: it is an unnecessary mutilation, a desecration of the image of God, and serving only the living. It is forbidden even if the person who died has asked for it. Since my mother's death, I've seen embalming done, as well as autopsies and cremations. I find embalming the most disturbing. In almost all cases, embalming has one purpose: it slows decomposition enough that cosmetic work can be done and a funeral can be held several days after death. It is not required by law. Don't believe it. The few exceptions involve a funeral delayed for a long period, or when a body is being transported by common carrier, like a train. Laws vary from state to state, but are far more liberal than many funeral directors would lead you to think. Embalming doesn't protect public health by preventing the transmission of disease except in rare cases, and doesn't destroy all bacteria or viruses. Dead bodies are not particularly dangerous most of the time, and disease transmission can be prevented with the same precautions used with sick people. The chemicals of embalming, principally formaldehyde, are toxic and dangerous, and they go into the ground with the body—hundreds of thousands of gallons of toxic chemicals every year.

I suppose the specialized vocabulary of many professions is

troubling to people outside those professions, since words are often used in unusual ways. Environmental engineers use a bomb calorimeter. A graphic designer is concerned with the bleed edge. A dairy farmer may do a teat dip. But the internal language of embalming is odd indeed because it is so clear. The vocabulary means just what it says. Embalmers use aspirators, separators, and arterial tubes. They may need eye replacers and mouth formers. Kelco makes a lip wax that is "formulated in a moderately loose consistency for applications to restore normal, dehydrated, blemished or traumatized lips and other soft tissue areas." A popular brand of pump is known as the Porti-Boy Mark V. The Esco company's "Primer" fluid offers "unsurpassed cosmetic effects and life-like color," because, the company literature explains, "maximum dilation of vessels ensures extensive penetration of arterial chemical and homogeneous distribution of natural color." Esco also offers "the original and still most powerful blood liquefying and mineral sequestering agent in the industry," for those more difficult cases. You can also buy a bone dust vacuum.

Embalming and "restorative art"—cosmetic work designed to make a corpse look like a living person—are sold to the public as a way to honor the dead person and preserve your positive memories of them. A school for restorers advertises that this skill helps family members by leaving them with "a peaceful eternal image of solace . . . by clearing the mind of perceived traumatic images of the deceased." Even talking to each other, they don't want to say *dead*. This is all about helping us, the living. "We at 'The Restorative Arts Academy' believe that the bereaved should, whenever possible, be faced with a deceased relative or friend who is presented in a visually acceptable manner, and in a safe environment. 'The Restorative Arts Academy' achieves this by not only return-

ing dignity to the deceased, but also by bringing a comforting reassurance to the bereaved at a time when most needed."

I know that my reaction to the practice is directly related to
my mother. But what better experience is there? I was her eldest
daughter, I was young, I had small children, I'd watched her decline through a fast-moving cancer. None of that was easy. Embalming interfered with my ability to accept her death. Directly.

The idea behind it—that we are comforted by not having to
see the dead body look dead; that we are somehow traumatized by
such a sight and able to find solace only by pretending they are still
alive—is not supported by any science or by history or anthropol-
ogy or our own experience. Embalming has been called the art of
complete denial.

After Carol died in the hospital's urgent roar, I didn't see her
body for a few days. She was kept cool but not embalmed, and
then dressed in one of her favorite hippie prairie dresses. Her
skin was hard and very cold when I kissed her. She looked dead.
She felt dead. And I began to shift from *Carol* to *Carol's body*.
After the viewing, the body was put into the muslin shroud, and
we buried Carol's body in her own little meadow, the place she'd
wanted to be. And I could feel the shift from *Carol's body* to *the
body*, *a body*, like the body of a weasel or rabbit. Like an antelope.
We lowered the body into the hole on the cardboard bier and
covered it with shovels of rich, dark dirt. Her husband planted a
tree at the head.

The poet and mortician Thomas Lynch gets angry when he
hears talk about embalming being a comfort to the living, or that
people shouldn't look at the body of the dead loved one because
it will spoil the memory. When someone tells Lynch they don't
want to look at the body because they want to remember a person

"the way he was," he suggests that they deal with "the way he is." Not looking is magical thinking. (In rare circumstances, such as a death from trauma, it may be reasonable to avoid full contact with the body. I would still suggest at least a distant view: a view that drives home the fact that the person has died, that what is left *is* a body.) Lynch doesn't find it helpful to say that the body is "merely a shell" and not the real person. Only a "frightened and well-meaning ignoramus" would try to comfort the grieving that way. Such words are just another way to deflect, to flinch at the blow that must be felt. Even if our personal belief is that the soul has left the body and the person we love is living in a noncorporeal place, not looking at the body doesn't make the loss of the living person easier to bear. "I'm an apostle of the present tense," he writes. "Seeing is the hardest and most helpful part."

At the moment of death, the blood in the body begins to settle with gravity. As the red blood cells start to break down, they release hemoglobin and stain the skin. This is called livor mortis, the discoloration of the body. A newly dead body turns gray, with dusky, bruised, and mottled areas. The face may be almost white or red or purple, while the back is livid and the chest is pale. Later a green cast spreads across the skin. These changes begin immediately after death. Livor mortis is the first visible sign of putrefaction, which proceeds in clear waves over months. In the instant after death, you are changed. Within days, you are unrecognizable.

Decomposition. Nothing can stop it.

Many cultures practice exposure of various kinds. In Europe and many other cultures, it was common practice to punish enemies and those seen as sinners by having their bodies thrown to dogs or scavengers—to deny a consecrated burial, to show the world the devastation of death. Other cultures consider exposure to be an honorable end. Traditional Tibetans practice what is called sky burial: the body is chopped into pieces and laid out for carrion eaters. The Zoroastrians place their dead bodies in a round raised structure known as a Tower of Silence. The thick, high walls are intended to protect the body from being degraded by water and fire. The bodies are laid on a rim inside, open to the air and the scavenger birds that perch on the walls. When they are reduced to a skeleton, attendants push the bones into the pit in the center.

I like the sound of this, exposure *to the elements*, to the world. It is what Perry wanted, and was not allowed to have. This is how countless people for countless years have returned to the earth. Our modern equivalent is the body farm, where corpses are laid out in a variety of conditions so that scientists can study natural decomposition, often for forensic research. Your body can be covered with a kind of cage if you prefer to be consumed primarily by insects, or you can be left out for the birds and small mammals, too.

Natural burial is simply the practice of burying a body without embalming, the way millions—billions!—of human bodies have been handled for uncounted centuries. (The Neanderthals started the practice.) Judaism and Islam share a tradition of burying a body in the earth as quickly as possible. If a coffin is used, it must have holes so the body touches the earth. But the image of burial in the ground is terrifying to many people: to be *food for worms*, a dreadful and seemingly unavoidable fate. Nigel Barley, an anthropologist who directed the British Museum's Museum of Mankind, writes of the nineteenth-century naturalist and vivid eccentric Charles Waterton, whose will protected the ducks from his estate after he died. Waterton knew that worms would eat him and that ducks eat worms and the thought could not be borne that anyone would eat the ducks. On the other hand, the Marquis de Sade insisted that he be buried in the forest in order to be eaten by trees.

You can slow things down a little if you're buried in a steel casket that costs thousands of dollars, with an interior that is "Chemically Treated to Resist Rust and Corrosion," with locking mechanisms, rubber gaskets, adjustable beds and waterproof lining. Walmart sells a casket "specially designed for a woman" with interior bedding in a light-pink velvet that is "soft to the touch," 18-gauge steel, and a welded bottom. Or you can rent a coffin and give it back after the funeral. You can be buried in a shroud. You can buy a coffin now that works as a bookcase, coffee table, or linen press until you don't need a linen press anymore, and then your friends can put it together the other way. You can paint a coffin, decorate it, draw on it, invite your friends to draw on it. You can fill the coffin with leaves and vines. You can be buried in willow, cardboard, paper, bamboo, or cotton.

You can buy a wooden coffin kit that can be put together without tools. You can get a biodegradable bespoke coffin: a police call box, a giant box of chocolates, a pile of autumn leaves, a set of armor, the deck of a starship. A golf bag. Leopard print. You don't have to bury a body *in* anything, but the urge to do so seems nearly universal. The formality of it, the slow, awkward, emotional work of fitting a body into a linen bag, or rolling the body back and forth into what has long been called a winding sheet—you can't do it alone. You need many hands for this work: the act drives home in a new way what has happened.

Jae Rim Lee went to MIT to study ways to redesign the human environment. She became particularly interested in waste, including that around human death. She studied conventional methods of embalming and burial, and then studied mycoremediation, the use of mushrooms to repair environmental damage. She founded the Infinity Burial Project and the Decompiculture Society, which are intended to help people get comfortable with what you might call postmortem change. Her Infinity Burial Suit (and soon the Infinity Burial Shroud) looks like one-piece pajamas: soft and roomy, with a hood, face mask, gloves, and footies. A line of white buttons looks stylish but is intended to ease dressing a body. The dark fabric is covered in white lines running along the edges like an embroidered vine impregnated with a bio mix of mushroom mycelium and other microorganisms. After burial, the mushrooms sprout and speed up decomposition. (The strains used are found around the world in order to avoid introducing invasive species.) The mushrooms also break down and neutralize toxins from the human body and—according to the Infinity Burial Project, which continues to study the process— increase the body's release of nutrients and energy to the soil.

You can also buy a mushroom suit for your pet.

There are hundreds of natural burial grounds in the United Kingdom, ranging from woods, parks, and meadows to a section of a traditional cemetery or churchyard. Natural burial is growing in popularity throughout the United States and Europe, where many cemeteries offer a particular section for the practice, and a few preserves have been created. The company Capsula Mundi makes a biodegradable egg designed to be buried beneath a tree planted above it. The small egg is intended for ashes and bone, and the larger egg for a whole body folded into a fetal position.

(You can also buy an egg for your pet.) Capsula is trying to sell more than an ecologically sensitive way to bury people; they are trying to sell the idea of a different kind of cemetery. The new natural burial ground is either a corner of a traditional cemetery of tombstones, or a distant, rural place. Imagine a city cemetery, there in the middle of the neighborhood, with trees of all types and sizes. Instead of orderly rows of tombstones, the graveyard is a rambling, woodsy place growing willy-nilly by the highway. Perhaps there are a few plaques here and there, a bench or two, but mostly there are trees, growing over eggs.

We tend to think of cemeteries as permanent places. Whether they feel like oases or wasted space depends on your point of view. Any given grave is really only temporary; as time goes by, many to a plot is common—sometimes more than one to a box. There is no end to the practice of reinventing and reusing gravesites. The headstone belongs to whoever bought it, but when you buy a site, you are usually buying a limited right to use the property: a "privilege," easement, or license that applies only as long as the place is a cemetery.

In the UK you can also lease what is called an "unpurchased grave," with no exclusive rights and no headstone. The landowner retains the right to bury someone else there as well. Prevailing law may say a grave is protected until a corpse is "dispersed," in commonly used language. The law may simply name a period of years—twenty, fifty, a hundred years. In Norway for a time in the 1950s, the law required all bodies be wrapped in plastic before burial. Eventually it was discovered that the bodies weren't decomposing fast enough to allow the graves to be reused in a timely manner. A gravedigger figured out that a lime solution would help, and he made a lot of money injecting cemeteries.

Even if the law says forever, there's no such thing. Just as a corpse is a unique object, a graveyard is a unique property. Ordinary real estate and corporate laws don't easily apply. Graves are seen to have inherently different qualities from other land. They are universal and indispensable and at the same time impermanent. In the United States, a government isn't allowed to absolutely prohibit the establishment of a graveyard, but it can set limits and even disinter bodies when public benefit seems to require it. In Alberta, Canada, a cemetery can be sold only to a religious group, a government, or another cemetery company, in an effort to keep cemeteries intact. If a graveyard is neglected—which happens eventually to all graves in time—or all the bodies are moved, the place is considered abandoned. An abandoned graveyard is no longer a graveyard, and can become something else. A park. A highway. Apartments. A vast reservoir. When the dams of the Tennessee Valley Authority were built, many graveyards were inundated. Most remains, such as they were, were moved first. Even pyramids crumble. Graves are lost, destroyed by landslides, floods, and sinkholes, emptied and turned into parking lots. There are countless bodies in our soil.

In 1786, the huge Les Innocents Cemetery of Paris was emptied, the bones and bodies and parts of bodies moved to the newly excavated catacombs. By then the ground was so saturated with corpses, with uncountable numbers of bodies festering in pits, that decomposition took place more or less in the open, and was often incomplete. The Church made a lot of money from burial fees and resisted government efforts to close the cemetery for many years, until the neighborhood was a wretched miasma and the basements of buildings began to collapse inward in piles of moldering carcasses. What an astonishing sight this spectacle of death must have been! For a long year—and, oh, it must have been a long year—Parisians were treated to nighttime caravans of rotting corpses carried through the city in carts. Enough fat was collected during the interment to make a good supply of candles and soap.

You can get a grave for free in Germany and Belgium, but only for twenty years or so. After that, your relatives will need to rent the space for you. If they don't, the remains are buried deeper or moved to a mass grave, and the site is used again. In London today, space for graves is so scarce that cemeteries have begun burying people under pathways and between existing graves. Both the government and the Church of England have warned people to expect graves to be reused—or, as the government likes to put it, "fully used"—after seventy-five years. At this point, there should be nothing left beyond a few bone fragments. The burial authorities can then open the grave to allow more burials in what is called the "lift and deepen" method: the remains are placed in a burlap sack to be reburied below the new coffin. Except for war graves, which are supposed to be kept in perpetuity, the maximum term for a grave is a hundred years. A loud minority is fighting the law in England. In Scotland, where a grave is called a *lair*, reuse is considered only after at least a hundred years, and only for a lair that appears abandoned. There was such resistance to reuse of graves in Sydney and Durban that efforts to do so were dropped. The problem is simply being pushed into the future.

In a city like Cairo, untold numbers of people have been buried over an eon. Graves last a long time in Egypt's dry climate, where the Cairo Necropolis stretches through the city for several miles. Millions of people are buried here in tombs and mausoleums of all sizes dating back to the seventh century AD. The graves are intact, but hundreds of thousands of people live among them and have for generations. Laundry hangs between the walls of tombs, children play inside the mausoleums, you can buy vegetables or get a shave next to a grave. Small homes have even been built in the narrow gaps. The necropolis is still active: people are still being buried there, while others are being born.

Nirvana Asia Ltd. of Hong Kong is the "largest integrated bereavement care provider in Asia," offering enormous and elaborate cemeteries in several countries. Nirvana combines graveyards, columbaria (air-conditioned, with "advanced laser lighting system and sound effect"), memorial tablet halls (with "dedicated chanting of mantra at scheduled times"), a "Baby Paradise" to help a child enter the afterlife freely, a burial ground carefully managed for maximum feng shui, and a cemetery for dogs and cats. But Hong Kong has been out of burial space for many years. Many people fulfill their responsibility to pay respects to dead ancestors by visiting a virtual grave; they can offer money or a roast pig by emoticon. Even public columbaria have a long waiting list now. A floating columbarium has been proposed to "offer serenity and breathtaking scenery with which inland sites can't compete," and the possibility of "sustained growth."

Space for graves is so scarce and expensive in Japan that large corporations may purchase a section of a cemetery and offer a site as an employee benefit. Japan also has webcams at several cemeteries, and you can subscribe to an online service to visit the virtual grave and use icons to offer flowers, fruit, and incense, a ladle of water or a glass of beer. A multistory columbarium retrieves individual urns robotically with the insertion of a key card. The Ruriden columbarium in Tokyo has 2,046 small altar niches in the walls of a quiet, dark room. Each holds a crystal Buddha statue illuminated with LED lights in different colors, representing a different drawer of ashes. When a person swipes their ID card, the appropriate statue lights up and blinks. This is not a cheap solution: a box for one person costs more than $6,000, and a small maintenance fee is required every year.

The main issue around the world is a lack of space. It has driven cemeteries up steep hills, into caves, and into the sky. Vertical cemeteries exist in several countries, the tallest being Brazil's Memorial Necrópole Ecumênica in Santos: fourteen stories tall, with twenty-five thousand burial units. The Necrópole is one of Santos's most popular tourist sites, with a snack bar on the roof and peacocks in the garden. This is not a cost-effective burial: even a three-year rental can cost tens of thousands of dollars here. The higher stories, with good views of the city, cost more. The three-year period reflects the typical decomposition time, after which families often have the remains removed to a cheaper, less advantageous unit.

The word *cemetery* comes from a Greek word for a sleeping place.

Shortly after Kyogen died, several of us bathed and dressed him at the hospital. We waited through the day in the hallucinatory clarity of loss. Finally, long after dark, we called the tissue donor service to take him away, many of us helping to slide the stiff, pale body into a thick black bag. Zipping it shut.

At the funeral home three days later, his body came out of the refrigerator in a plastic coverall meant to catch leaking fluids. The limbs were soft and ragged where bones had been removed. His chest was sunken from the removal of the heart valves. The skin felt like damp wax. We had to dress him in a white funeral kimono over the coverall. As we rolled and pulled and tugged, the body gurgled and sighed, and the room was perfumed with odd smells. For a moment I felt one with every broken human being consigned to struggle with the fact of change: the immeasurable wonder and disaster of change. We billions, who love and cry and try to understand.

Do not turn away.

In time, the same thing happens to all bodies, no matter what we do. Embalmed bodies decompose, just more slowly and in a different pattern. Insects don't seem to like formaldehyde much, and will focus on the parts of the body with the least chemical saturation. This is often the buttocks. Decomposition rates vary with season, temperature, moisture, the quality of the soil, the depth of the burial, the kind of casket, and other factors, but insects and animals usually make short work of things. A buried body may take years. Cremation is just a kind of very fast decomposition. The results are more or less the same.

Maggots can reduce the weight of an exposed human body by 50 percent in a few weeks. There are several waves of insects in a decomposing body, colonizing in a strict sequence. The first wave is blowflies and houseflies of certain species; they begin to arrive within minutes of death. Their bodies are beautiful and glass-like, shimmering greens and blues with warm, deep-red eyes. They lay eggs in dark, warm corners and the larvae quickly hatch and begin to eat. A dead body is alive in a new way, a busy place full of activity. At times the body seems to move of its own accord from their motion.

Eventually, other species of blowflies and houseflies arrive. The corpse begins to blacken and soften. (Corpses at this stage are called "wet carrion" by biologists.) The meat on which the maggots feed begins to liquefy and runs like melting butter. "We here witness the transfusion of one animal into another," the great entomologist Jean-Henri Fabre wrote. By the time these larvae have fallen off into the soil to pupate, a third wave of flies arrives: fruit flies and drone flies and others, flies that prefer the liquids. Toward the end, the cheese skipper appears and carefully cleans the bones of the remnants of tendons and connective tissue.

In Seattle, an interdisciplinary team is doing research into the ultimate natural burial, the eventual result of all burials made into a social choice: compost. Recompose (formerly called the Urban Death Project) is a public benefit corporation in partnership with several universities, foundations, architects, soil scientists, and lawyers. A two-year pilot project involving six cadavers showed proof of concept: in the proper mix of materials, oxygenation, and moisture, the bodies completely decomposed in five to eight months. A larger pilot project at the University of Washington's Pullman campus began in the fall of 2017. This phase is intended to answer questions about pathogens, heavy metals, controls, and seasonal variations. So many people are interested in donating their body to this project that the organization has had to limit donations to people reasonably expected to die during the next year of research.

As the method is perfected, the organization will move toward building a prototype building and creating legal language for legislation. The goal is a large-scale system in which cities could receive and manage bodies in a formal, almost ritualized way, and recover fertile soil for use in parks and landscapes. The company uses the term *recomposition*, and writes cheerfully of people being "recomposed"—which is what actually happens, what happens to every one of us whether we agree or not. We are decomposed, compounded, dissolved, disappearing, reappearing; the air takes a piece from here and the soil a fleck from there. That speck of memory, released into this carbon atom and that drop of water, runs into the earth. A little protein, a bit of sugar, a pinch of wisdom, hard gained: it all softens and combines until new life is made from pieces of the past.

The idea of knowing that I could become compost, could be truly used after death, is deeply satisfying. I contemplate my ordinary, imperfect, beloved body. I contemplate the bodies of my beloveds: individual, singular, unique, irreplaceable people, their skin and eyes and mouths and hands. I consider their skin riddled and bristling with that seething billow of maggots. I consider the digestion of their eyes and the liquefaction of those hands (my hands, my eyes), the rending of flesh and muscle by beak and claw. The evolution of the person into the thing, into meat and wet carrion and eventually into a puddle, into new flies, into earth and root. What better vision of the fullness of birth and the fullness of death than the maggot and the carrion eater? "Placed in her crucibles, animals and men, beggars and kings are one and all alike," wrote Fabre. "There you have true equality, the only equality in this world of ours: equality in the presence of the maggot." Even the Buddha: they came and turned him into juice and soil, and the Buddha flowed gloriously like cream into the ground.

More than half of India's population lives within a few hundred miles of the river Ganges—Ganga, the Mother. In Varanasi, a stretch of riverbank several miles long is divided into more than a hundred ghats, broad staircases that lead to the water, each ghat the plaza of a miniature neighborhood, catering to different needs. People bathe at dawn every day, reciting prayers. They come to do laundry, to visit, to make offerings, to flirt, to get a shave and haircut, buy fruit, commit crimes, gossip, sell betel, ride a ferry. People fall in love along the river, smoke, play cards, meet friends. There are always people here, and always wandering cows and feral dogs and rowboats and ferries slowly sliding by.

The first time I came to Varanasi, I walked the entire length of the ghats over the course of several days. The boatmen lounged against the pilings, their agents calmly patrolling the crowds: "Madam, boat?" "Boat, Madam?" "Boat?" Boats could be had at any spot along the way, for an hour or a day, to go up or go down, to cross the river to the floodplain where people buy chips, splash in the shallows, or rent horses for a holiday ride. Boat prices are open to negotiation, varying with the current, the weather, the time of day, and the boatman's mood. Many seem to hope that negotiations will fail.

People come to the Ganges to die, because, in Hindu belief, to be cremated by the Ganges is to be released all at once from the cycle of suffering and reincarnation. (Certain people do not need to be cremated, such as unwed girls. They need merely to be sunk into the holy river.) The two burning ghats, as they are called, are hard to miss; a fog of smoke hovers over each of them. "Boat, Madam?" is sometimes followed by "See the burning ghat?" The cremations are popular with tourists.

Some people watch from boats because visitors are not entirely welcomed on the burning ghat itself and photographs are forbidden. Occasionally a local will try to shoo the casual observer along, but the ghats are always crowded with sightseers, Indian and foreign both. The main one is surrounded by enormous towering constructions of firewood as tall as multistory buildings and smells of heavy, oily smoke. The sites are never still; there are always fires burning, perhaps a dozen or more at a time, each built on the ashes of previous fires so that the entire plaza has become a pillow of ash, fine dust floating up with every step. In a hot city, this is the hottest place, oven heat rolling in waves across the steps and along the walkways between the columns of wood. For all of the watchers and the endless burning, it is quiet: the crackling of fire, the thud of falling wood, the murmured prayers.

Men work around the clock, building and tending and stirring fires. Here a dying fire, there a body fully engulfed, a blackened skull facing the sky. Now and then, dry-eyed mourners carry a body wrapped in cloth and draped in chrysanthemums down to the water, trailed by the eldest son. He steps awkwardly over the ash, wearing only a loincloth, his head newly shaved and looking like he'd really like to get back to work at the bank. The body is dipped into the water. While it dries, the family purchases firewood and the pyre is built. Then the body is laid on top, and in a matter of moments the flames begin to rise. The fire will burn for hours. I sit for a long time on the steps, taking notes in a small book, my camera and phone carefully hidden. I turn away several young men who try to hit me up for donations to a fake hospice nearby. A small dog pads around, pawing at the ash. I watch a blackened body surrounded by flames that are almost transparent against the bright day. A leg is sticking out of the burning shroud, slowly shrinking in the flame until suddenly the foot falls off and rolls to the side. A fire tender pushes it back into the flames with a stick.

Cremation is one of the most common methods for disposing of a corpse in the world. Almost everyone in Japan is cremated. There are thousands of crematories in China, more than
a thousand in Europe. Throughout India and Nepal, seven million people are burned on open pyres every year. In 2016, more
than half of Americans who died were cremated. Cremation is
cheaper than a traditional burial, and some people want to be
free of the funeral home folderol. The vocabulary of coffins is
protection, *defense*, *peace of mind*. The language of cremation is *af-
fordability*, *simplicity*, *ease*.

Don't try this at home. A cremation oven runs as hot as 1,800
degrees Fahrenheit. Few bonfires reach the temperatures needed.
The human body is wet, a loose collection of watery cells, about
85 percent moisture. In the oven, the coffin or shroud burns away
first. The intense heat quickly evaporates the body's water and
the suddenly dry skin and hair ignite. Everything soft chars, shriv-
els, and burns away. The abdomen may swell and burst. On occasion, the chamber has to be opened to reposition the body for
a more thorough burn. Metal may melt but not combust: gold
fillings, jewelry, the rods and pins of a rebuilt femur. Gradually
the skeleton is exposed, cooking until the bones are friable and
begin to crumble. At the end of cremation, about 5 percent of
the body is left.

Perhaps one day we will collectively throw up our hands and
decide cremation is just too dirty. Crematoria are considered incinerators, in the same category as municipal waste and hazardous
waste incinerators. The cremation of an average adult requires
more than two million BTU an hour of energy. (To compare, a
gallon of gasoline provides about 124,000 BTU.) The pyres of
India and Nepal use up more than fifty million trees every year

and create a significant fraction of the particulate pollution of this very polluted region. Cremation releases a number of dangerous compounds into the atmosphere along with greenhouse gases. Mercury from dental fillings is vaporized in cremation and released in significant amounts, and mercury has been shown to accumulate in soil near crematoria. Quantities of persistent toxic chemicals known as polychlorinated dibenzo-p-dioxins (PCDDs) and polychlorinated dibenzofurans (PCDFs) are also released. The real environmental effects have been little studied by any government, but a few limited surveys in England showed increased birth defects and stillbirths in the vicinity of crematoria.

Despite the many costs, for a grieving person cremation can have a kind of stark beauty. George Bernard Shaw watched his mother's body enter the crematorium, feet-first. "The feet burst miraculously into streaming ribbons of garnet colored lovely flame, smokeless and eager, like pentecostal tongues," he wrote, "and as the whole coffin passed in it sprang into flame all over; and my mother became that beautiful fire." If you pay attention, burning has a blunt impact that is hard to deny.

A few days after Kyogen died, after he became a donor and we dressed his body in the formal white kimono, hundreds of people processed around the open cardboard casket. Then the casket was sealed, and the people who had been closest to him walked the coffin across the parking lot into the crematorium and pushed it into the oven. His widow pushed a red button, and the flames came on in a great whoosh of sound. As I walked to my car, I glanced up at the crematorium chimney. I couldn't see the smoke in the sun-bright sky. But, looking down, I saw its shadow dancing and wavering across the asphalt.

The next day a few of us returned to sort through the bones, saved for us in a big metal tray. The tray lay on top of the crushing machine used to turn leftover bone into ash, the coarse material known as cremains that are typically put in an urn and given to the family. But you can have the bones. Bones are not smooth. They are notched and grooved, and each notch means something, represents a piece of the life. The furrows of bones show us where things attached, how the body was woven into one. These bones were cocooned in muscle, nerve, and blood; they were leverage and core. This bone held weight, all the weight of the body, and ran and jumped and rolled. This bone gave form to the delicate tendons of the hand. This bone protected the heart, the liver, the lungs. This bone defended the brain. These are warriors, these bones. They are good to see. Kyogen's bones were friable but easy to recognize, and we could fit a few together like pieces of a jigsaw puzzle: vertebrae, part of the pelvis, small bones from the fingers, pieces of rib, a segment of skull. I keep several small pieces in a box. Memento mori. Remember, you will die.

Ashes can be scattered (almost anywhere, but watch the wind), buried, or kept in a jar on the shelf. But you can also have Mom made into stained glass. Mail yourself to a good friend; the United States Postal Service doesn't mind. Be made into a matched set of 240 pencils. (Talk about writing a life story.) Stuff a teddy bear. You can become an hourglass. ("They cannot be exactly timed, due to the consistency of the cremains.") Get added to an artificial coral reef. Be compressed into a diamond. Be mixed in with tattoo ink or paint. Be pressed into a vinyl record. You can mix Dad into fireworks. And you can load your father into shotgun shells, which is advertised by the Holy Smoke company in Alabama as being "eco-friendly." The bullets can be made in "almost any caliber or gauge of ammunition" so your family can "honor" you by shooting your ashes at "sporting clays or live birds." You can "have the peace of mind of knowing that you can continue to protect your home and family even after you are gone."

Nigel Barley reports that "a museum colleague has decreed that his ashes shall be flung in the eyes of the Trustees of the British Museum."

I live in a coastal state, and a lot of people here think about burial at sea. (Preferably a Viking funeral, the burning boat bobbing slowly out with the tide, flames over sea until the boat sinks and the body is carried away.) Sea burial is usually more complicated and expensive than earth burial. The body must be ferried out at least three miles to international waters, weighted, and dropped into a depth of at least six hundred feet. A fair amount of paperwork is required. If you are a veteran or the spouse of a Navy or Coast Guard veteran, burial at sea is free, but the paperwork is complicated and the scheduling is slow. Slow as in months, pending the position of ships and their maneuvers.

Margaret Drabble is in her late seventies now and making plans. She has asked to be cremated and "not buried in the cold earth." She wonders about sea burial: "The thought of being devoured underwater is strangely attractive to me, but I think it's hard to arrange, and I won't want to be a nuisance." I want to tell Drabble that sea burial is quite a nuisance, and that if she dislikes the cold ground, she won't be happy with the sea. Decomposition goes faster in warm water than in soil. But in cold water—which is all there is at six hundred feet—bodies go through fairly dramatic chemical changes that most people will find at least as distressing as ordinary decomposition, and they are not exactly devoured, at least not in a timely way. The government of India releases thousands of turtles into the Ganges every year to help eat the remains of all those bodies.

The word *resomation* is taken from the Greek *resomer*, meaning "rebirth of the body." It is also sometimes called biocremation. One of the funeral homes offering this in the United States prefers the term *dissolution*, which resonates for me. The body is quickly reduced to ash through a process known as alkaline hydrolysis. The chemical reaction is similar to what happens to a buried body, but, as with cremation, it happens very fast. Alkaline hydrolysis has long been used to dispose of dead livestock; it is used by a few medical schools to dispose of cadavers when they are no longer useful for research. The body is placed into a closed drum. Instead of fire, the body is bathed in water and potassium hydroxide and heated to around 350 degrees Fahrenheit. Over a period of a few hours, the flesh and organs are reduced to liquid. The cleaned skeleton becomes powdery and can be crushed into ash. Resomation is much cleaner than cremation, uses significantly less fuel, and releases no mercury vapor. Such an unexpected melding of water and fire—fire without flame.

A Scottish company called Resomation Ltd developed the technology for human funerals. It is currently available in several locations in the United Kingdom and legal in nine American states. Legislation is pending in six more, not counting a number of exceptions already in place for medical schools. When the first funeral home in the United States started offering resomation, the founder of the company told a reporter, "Let's face it—there's no nice way to go. You have to go from what looks like a human person to ash and bone, whether you get there by flame or decomposition.

"If you stood in front of a cremation, with the flames and heat, it seems violent. You go next door and the resomation is quiet. It's stainless steel and clinical and sterile. It seems nicer." Perhaps not exactly *nice*; the liquid left over may come to as much as a hundred gallons. In many cases, the liquid is considered safe for sewer systems and perhaps even agriculture, but in other cases the pH is too high.

I feel comfortable with the idea of my body decomposing. I don't believe that "I" will experience this in any way—back to Epicurus and his nothing to fear. I've certainly seen my body change in dramatic ways over sixty years. Eight years old, chasing a lizard in the high, dry grass of the hills above town. Pregnant. Bench-pressing my own weight. Recovering from surgery. I've been small and big, strong and weak, smooth and textured. I've lost parts of my body and other parts are damaged; a few parts have been fixed and others shored up against time. The idea that this body will gradually disintegrate altogether seems obvious. But resomation, which is simply the same process happening quickly, is a little weird. Would I want a bottle of fluid, a jar of you, sloshing and heavy? But you and I are mostly fluid, after all. Resomation liquid is not kindred to bone but to the smoke and vapor of cremation. That I can be turned into slurry and ash in a few hours can only be a spur to self-reflection. And the jar of you or me won't pollute the planet; we can water the plants instead.

The Swedish company Promessa invented the technique they call Promession, in which the body is cryogenically frozen at −320 degrees Fahrenheit, turning the entire body into crystal. When the body is vibrated, it dissolves into tiny crystalline particles. The particles are gathered and freeze-dried, removing the remaining water. The dried particles are then treated to remove metals such as mercury. According to the company, a 155-pound body will leave 44 pounds of crystals. If they are buried in a biodegradable container at a shallow depth, the remains decompose into soil in six to eighteen months.

I felt like I'd come across something new when I heard about Promession. It's a bit technically demanding—not exactly do-it-yourself like natural burial—but may be the most aesthetically pleasing body disposal method around, a fairly clean way to get people to stop using formaldehyde and 18-gauge steel, or millions of BTUs. Right now it is legal only in Sweden and Scotland, but Promessa has partnered with people around the world and is offering training in the hope that more countries will approve the technology.

You can donate your entire body for research or education. You can donate just your brain, which is especially useful for research into dementia, no matter what your cognitive state was at the time of death. In some states, an unclaimed body may be claimed by a medical school, a university, or even an individual physician for dissection and research. (This includes prisoners, historically the most common source of cadavers.) Cadaveric tissue is used in countless ways. Whole cadavers are used to teach anatomy, but the uses of a whole cadaver are manifold: studying the efficacy of helmets, testing new surgical procedures, designing a new space capsule. The Army uses cadavers for research into "impacts, blasts, ballistics testing, crash testing and other destructive forces." If you can imagine a use for a cadaver, it's probably true.

Whole-body donation needs to be done well in advance, and every medical school has its own policy. Don't forget osteopathic and chiropractic colleges, which tend to go wanting. A school can reject a donated body if it's not appropriate. My local medical school requires bodies to weigh between 100 and 200 pounds and to be free of HIV, tuberculosis, hepatitis, and Creutzfeldt-Jakob disease. The body must not have been autopsied or have extensive trauma. Bodies and parts are cremated or resomated and the remains returned to families, usually within three years. But once a corpse is dissected or used in experiments, it may be seen to have value and thus become property. No one owns a body, exactly, and bodies can't make wishes or have rights, but tissue, once used in research, occupies another position. Everything from cells to anatomical specimens can be claimed.

You can opt to have your body displayed. The whole body or its parts can be preserved for a classroom or museum exhibit. The most pristine way to do this is plastination. It's a new method, but an old idea—an ideal, in fact. Anatomists have tried to preserve bodies in various ways for centuries using honey, tanning, alcohol, or the injection of fixatives. Lifelike models of dissected bodies have also been made for hundreds of years, many from wax molded onto real skeletons. Plastination is the zenith of this effort to preserve and display a body in the most exact way possible. The corpse undergoes a complex process involving embalming, dissection, an acetone bath, freezing, and then a polymer bath and hardening. (This is not a particularly eco-friendly practice.) The result of plastination is one of the odder objects in the world: an anatomically precise specimen that is only fractionally organic. A body that both is and is not a body.

Plastination is still quite controversial, and the displays have been banned in several places. (The use of the bodies of prisoners from China was widely criticized, and the company states it has made changes to avoid this. At this time, the German headquarters for Body Worlds states that they have a list of more than thirteen thousand volunteer donors.) "The preservation of human bodies by plastination converts humans into objects," writes Catherine Belling, a literature and medicine scholar. She calls such models "metameat," a "hybrid" thing with "the genetic properties of flesh and the inedible staying power of polyurethane." Belling is particularly bothered by this "inedible" quality: the body turned into an inorganic object. She wants the body to decompose, to be, as it were, eaten.

Tarris Rosell, a professor of theology, is disturbed by the models' apparent activity. Plastinated bodies are positioned running or throwing, bending and twisting. "They are the playing or working dead, perpetually posed without repose, positioned without disposition," he writes. "For those who subscribe to an ethics of bodily repose, this treatment of human corpses is morally repugnant."

I saw the Body Worlds exhibit several years ago at the local science museum. It was stunning and spooky and beautiful. A head had been stripped of everything but its circulatory system, and the arteries, veins, and capillaries wove in an intricate tangle as dense as delicate crochet. Bodies taken down to muscle revealed the precise tension of ligaments, the leverage of weight on the rope of tendon and bone. The model of a man held his own skin in his hand, presenting it to the world—an image created by anatomical modelers for centuries. I was moved by the exhibit, especially taken as a whole: rooms filled with human movement, humans posed and humans looking at humans posed, biological wonder seen by an audience wondering in its own biology. I felt gratitude.

The mortician and poet Thomas Lynch wants to be buried. He knows what he wants his funeral to look like: "I want a mess made in the snow so that the earth looks wounded, forced open, an un-willing participant. Forgo the tent." He tells those who will come to mourn to "stand openly to the weather," and suggests that it would be good if they were cold. "See it to the very end. Avoid the temptation of tidy leave taking." Lynch took the title of this essay, "Tract," from a poem by William Carlos Williams, in which Williams gives instructions for a funeral. He explains what the hearse and driver should look like, how they should move. He prescribes an old cart, a single horse, a muddy road. He tells the mourners,

> Go with some show
> of inconvenience;

11

Grieving

We are left with the impulse. You reach for a glass that isn't there, and your hand swishes through empty air. You step down and the stair is missing and you stumble into space. Grief is the frozen moment when you pat your pocket for your keys, the pocket where you always put your keys, and your keys aren't there. The intensely familiar is gone—not just a person, but a habit. Gone. When I do this, that happens. When I say this, you answer. When I reach for you, there you are. And then I am reaching, and nothing, nothing is there. The true has become false.

Grief is disruption. The sound of a footstep on the porch evokes the old world, the other life, and it is only the mail carrier and the new life rushes back. My mother has been gone from my life for more than thirty years, but I hear her voice sometimes when I talk, and I see her in the mirror now and then—sidelong, unexpected glances. There she is. And I think, *I should call Mom and tell her about that.* Grief recurs and spins, a Möbius strip of memory going on and on in a loop. You aren't in denial about the death. You just keep remembering that it happened.

I had spoken to Carol on Christmas Eve. Two days later I had to go to work. A heavy snowfall, the same storm that had kept me from visiting Carol before the holiday, had closed the clinic. Tony, the doctor, and I were doing home visits in his pickup. My cell phone rang as we were parking in front of a patient's home. I saw Carol's name on the screen and picked up quickly and said hello.

"We lost her," David said. And this didn't make sense for a moment: *She's right there. What are you talking about?* He started to explain—the difficulty, the trip through the snow, the emergency room. I stepped out of the truck and fell down in the snow.

Until that day, until I felt the violence of this pain, the way it seemed to shred my skin, I didn't quite know that one really does collapse. I hadn't felt it with my mother; she'd been unconscious for days and I'd anticipated her death for a long time and so the collapse was a slow one. I had time to reach back and find a chair, as it were. I think of our long line of ancestors, name after name into an almost infinite past. I imagine them gurgling and loosening their hold on the furs in the candlelight, or dropping like a stone while chopping wood. I imagine the collapse, the shock, the sorrowful people preparing them for the soil and the fire. Sometimes I feel the naked commonness of our species. I knelt in the snow, holding the phone, and saying, "What? What?" Tony looking at me.

You flinch. You know it will hurt and you know it will hurt for a long time. You touch it like an abscessed tooth and skid away. Grief lives in the body. MRI studies show that a grieving brain has a pattern unlike other emotions. Most of the time, an emotion lights up parts of the brain, but grief is distributed everywhere, into areas associated with memory, metabolism, visual imagery, and more. Grief can make you sick; it can be brutal, even deadly. One is coming to grips with what *forever* means. And we don't do that all at once and we don't do it one day at a time but for one minute and then another minute and then another. Don't ever say: *Get over it, move on. She's in a better place now.*

Grief is full of surprises. Anything is possible. You may feel unreal, drugged. Numbness is one of the most common sensations. You may be calm or excited or enraged. You may be so relieved, relieved that it's over, the illness, the injury, the weeks and months that turned into a waiting room in which no one's number was ever called. Then you are overwhelmed with guilt for feeling relieved. It's all very confusing: hard, difficult work. Work! No one tells you that grief is like a long march in bad weather. You're forgetful and find it hard to make decisions and have no interest in the decisions you are being asked to make. You lose track of time, because time changes, too, shifting and slowing, speeding up, stopping altogether. An hour becomes an elastic, outrageously delicate thing, disappearing or stretching beyond comprehension. One is deranged, in the truest sense of the word: everything arranged has come apart.

In grief, I have baked a cake in the middle of the afternoon and left out the sugar and not been able to figure out why it tasted so bad. I have watched a lot of television and stayed up very late and had many strange dreams that evaporated in the morning light. I have awoken each morning to the shock renewed, to think, *He died. She died.* Decades of Buddhist practice and many hours at the bedsides of the dying, and all that these have given me in my weeks of acute grief is not acceptance but awareness of not accepting. I can see my disbelief for what it is. I think, *He died,* and then take a deep breath and reset my compass to this new world. This new world in which a person who had immense influence on my life does not exist. This vacuum. I am dead, too; the me that lived in the other world, the world where she was, died. The me who knew instinctively where he was and suffered a little when he was far away died. Who am I now? All the possibilities of the life of that former me, the me-with-her, are extinguished. Grieving, one is thrust into a new life—an unwelcome life. It takes time for that life to become familiar, to feel like the life you are actually living. You can be happy again, but you can never be happy and the same again.

A friend of mine called the numbness that falls over you immediately after a death "like swimming in thick gelatin mixed with cotton candy and filled with webs and you're trying to push it aside and you can't push it aside." You may not remember much of the days after a death. I remember little about my mother's funeral, though I did a lot of the organizing. I remember the fight my brother and sister had afterward, the casseroles on the dining table. But I don't remember how we got the church ready or if there were flowers or what my father did that day or what I wore. I remember sitting in the back yard late that night, drinking bourbon with her friend Hutch, the music teacher who had been my bandleader in middle school. We were drinking and watching the stars, and I was so tired. *Nothing will be the same,* I thought, leaning back in the chaise longue as though into a pool, sinking into the warm dark night. I remember that.

You have trouble remembering details while the rest of the world forgets the big event. People are almost surprised that you haven't forgotten, too. What we miss is often the most mundane thing. How she folded a towel. The sound of his foot on the porch. Her handwriting. I keep a recipe card from my mother's collection on my bulletin board because she had beautiful handwriting and she tried to instill that in me, with little luck. You miss the snore that used to annoy you so. The scent of soap. The pat on the bottom. Small, ordinary things that no one else misses. You can't say to a grieving person who is suddenly frantic about not being able to do the laundry together that doing the laundry isn't important. Only the grieving person knows why it *is* so important, why not being able to do the laundry together is an immeasurable loss. The loss may be accepted in time, but this isn't the same as "getting over it." There are so many things not to say now: *At least your mother and father are together again. He's in a better place. You'll marry again someday.* (People say such stupid things. I just heard about a person who was told her daughter's death was just the result of her karma. Consider asking a neutral friend to stay with you during the funeral as a stupidity monitor. Let them be the gentle bouncer: to say that you need to be alone, need to step out, can't do any more hugging, don't want to hold any more hands.)

We are trained about crying from a very young age. In the West, we often judge open grief as unseemly, "hysterical"—yet a stoic person is judged as unfeeling. Men and women receive wildly different messages about tears. How and when we cry is conditioned by our entire experience and has nothing to do with whether our hearts are broken. Some people cry, some don't. Some cry a lot, others a little. Some cry for a long time, others briefly. The tears of grief are structurally different from the tears of laughter and happiness; they are literally of a different shape. There is no prescription for tears. What not to say: *Don't cry; it will make you feel worse.* Don't say: *Why aren't you crying? It will make you feel better.*

Crying is neither necessary nor sufficient. The grief counseling partners John W. James and Russell Friedman write, "During our grief recovery seminars, when someone starts crying, we gently urge them to 'talk while you cry.'

"The emotions are contained in the words the griever speaks, not in the tears that they cry. What is fascinating to observe, is that as the thoughts and feelings are spoken, the tears usually disappear, and the depth of feeling communicated seems much more powerful than mere tears. . . . Tears [can] become a distraction from the real pain."

Regret is inevitable. Not one of us has lived a life without error. Grief is remorseful. Grief is angry. Angry at the disease: at the terrible choices that had to be made, at the stolen days. Angry at the accident, the mistake, the stupidity of death. Angry at the dead person. *How dare you go away? How dare you leave me alone?* Angry at everyone involved, everyone who didn't stop death. The motorcyclist came over the crest of the hill way too fast, straight into a car pulling out into traffic. I was mad at him even when I was trying to get his heart to beat again: the risk, the damage done to the other driver, to the neighbors, to his friend, his family, to me. We long to blame someone. Why wasn't she wearing a seat belt? Why didn't he tell anyone he had chest pain? Why wouldn't he quit smoking?

Anger can be a way for the survivor to deal with the fear of surviving: *How do I go on? How do I live now?* Weeks after Carol's death, her husband kept reviewing the last day, questioning everything, his decisions and the actions of the doctors and nurses. He felt rage at the universe's "utter dumbness," he wrote. "Mouthbreathing doofuses. When I go into town and see them walking around alive and Carol died, it is totally stupid."

Religion doesn't fix grief. (Don't say: *God always has a plan.*) Explanations don't fix it, advice doesn't fix it, sharing doesn't fix it. All these things may help immensely, but grief is not a disease to be cured. Grief is a wound not unlike that from a knife or a bludgeon. The injury will heal in time, leaving a scar, but the tissue is never quite the same. One moves forward, changed. The Roman philosopher Seneca said, "All your sorrows have been wasted on you if you have not yet learned how to be wretched."

Grief is not orderly or predictable. There is no schedule. I have seen people in their seventies weeping over the loss of a parent in their nineties. One of my students lost her husband this winter. He died at the breakfast table while she was out of town visiting her own elderly mother. A well-meaning person told her that her grief should last two months. More like two years, she thinks, but who knows? My student writes, "Every thought I have is based on assumptions that are now out of date. That's why it takes a long time." Grief lasts as long as it lasts. Sometimes it lasts a lifetime. It may evolve and may even cease to be painful, but we are changed. The poet Jack Gilbert wrote: "He manages like somebody carrying a box / that is too heavy." The man adjusts his arms and hands, holds the weight in different ways, shifting when his muscles tire. He keeps finding new ways to carry that heavy, heavy box, "so that / he can go on without ever putting the box down."

Grief is the internal experience of loss. Mourning is its outward expression. Together we call this bereavement, a wonderful word. Its root comes from the Old English *berēafian*, which means to rob.

James Wilce, an anthropologist, studies lamentation, the impassioned cries of the grieved, what he calls "spontaneous tuneful texted weeping" or "melodic wailing." Lamentation is found around the world. In the last several years, he has studied a form practiced by the Karelian people of Finland. The Finnish Lament Society (Äänellä Itkijät ry) has revived the traditional practice and teaches it in workshops in a reinvented form, explicitly intended as a kind of self-help technique, useful for any loss. Wilce describes it as a singsong speaking, or "weep-and-speak," done in a particular kind of intonation, a kind of music built out of pain—a cracked and lonesome sound. The laments tell the life story of the dead person and help to wake up those who have already died, so they can come and meet the newly deceased. Wilce has attended several of the trainings, and found that his old grief about a sister who died in childhood was met more completely by the lamentation than it had been by years of therapy. He said of the experience, "Be prepared to be overcome."

As individual as grief is, taking its own path like the rivulets of rain along a glass, mourning has many forms. Islamic culture frowns on public shows of grief; a little quiet crying for a few days should be enough. Too much mourning can be seen as a rejection of one's destiny and submission to God. Some Muslims don't buy life insurance; they believe that it is forbidden to trade something you don't own, and your life belongs to God. Islam posits God's mercy, regardless of our predisposition to evil behavior. Death is not a tragedy if you are going to heaven. In other cultures, the bereft will fall prostrate, shake his fists at heaven, beat his chest. People slice their skin, cut off or tear out their hair, tear their clothes to pieces, or wear special clothing for the rest of their lives. A person may be expected to get a particular kind of tattoo.

In traditional Jewish tradition, mourners tear a piece of clothing in a particular way and wear the torn clothing for the seven days of mourning called shiva. For a week after the death, the family is cared for by friends and neighbors. They sit together, often on low stools instead of chairs. Men don't shave; women wear no

makeup. They may not bathe and are not supposed to study the
Torah, except the portions related to grief, because to study the
Torah is a pleasant thing to do. During these seven days, the world
is set aside, held apart, while those left behind remember—set
aside, that is, except for countless telephone calls and visitors and
even emails sent by friends and relatives, each requiring a personal
response. An Orthodox friend of mine finds shiva a great trial.
(She refers to the endless stream of people as a kind of "assault"
to those who like to be alone.) I am sure that sitting shiva is boring and the neighbors are intrusive and annoying, the stools are
uncomfortable, and everyone begins to smell a little bad. But this
setting aside of all things, surrendering power to the community
for a time, seems wise in its way. Maybe it should be a trial; it is
a container of discomfort, built by others, a labor giving birth to
a new life.

I worked for several years on an oncology unit. One evening
I had an old Tongan woman as my patient. She was dying. By luck
or forethought, she'd been admitted alone to a double room.
Through the course of the night, many relatives gathered: at least
twenty big, cheerful Tongans crowded in, catching up and gossiping and sharing McDonald's takeout and laughing. My patient lay
silently, eyes closed, never speaking. Late in the evening, a young
woman found me at the desk and said, "I think she's gone." I listened to her chest. No heartbeat, no breath. I waited a moment
to be sure and then looked at the room full of people and said,
"She has died."

Never have I been so impressed with the fact that mourning is
a social experience. One by one, each sister, cousin, and nephew,
every relative, came to the side of the bed, knelt, and cried loudly
for a few minutes. Then each stood and turned away and went

directly back to gossiping, laughing, and sharing food. This went on for a few hours, until every person had taken a turn.

I appreciated the ritual acknowledgment that the event was momentous, that it deserved recognition even from distant relatives who may not be feeling personal grief. I have wanted to wail, to cover the mirrors and wear only black for months. James Wilce makes the specific point that Finnish lamentation is not "stereotypical, modern, Protestant, or dry-eyed." Which is exactly my heritage: hooded, a little taciturn, tight-lipped.

I don't remember much about my mother's funeral. It was the middle of the afternoon, and people were solemn, squeezing my father's elbow, patting my hand, without a word. A few dabbed at their eyes, but no one was crying. I sat with my father and my brother and sister in the front row. Then the young Lutheran pastor came forward casually and put his hand on the casket, as though on the shoulder of a friend. "This woman," he said to the church, which to my surprise was filled with people, "this was a *good* woman." I had been filled with crying, and crying wouldn't come. Until then I'd been calm. But the laying of hands on my mother's coffin, this expression of the intimacy of peers and maybe friends, the loving acknowledgment of my shy, plain, charitable mother's life, was too much for even my pride. That's when I was finally able to cry; I filled the church with sobs. Finally.

Try not to say: *You shouldn't dwell on the past.* Grief is a story that must be told, over and over. Very few people know how to listen to a grieving person without in some way trying to shut down or control the strong emotion. ("A grieving acquaintance is a shy person's nightmare," says Lindy West.) Because it is hard for others to listen, the grieving tell each other the story of their losses, over and over. There are so many things not to say. What are the things *to* say? *I love you. I'm so sorry.* And one of the best things to say is *Do you want to talk? I would be glad to listen to the story.* The story of how you met, of what he was like as a child, of her favorite food, of that trip you took together to Iceland, why he liked that blue plaid shirt so much, what the last moments were like. Whatever story you want to tell.

We want to tell the story, our story, and we want to know the rest of the story—not just the life story, but the story of the death. There can be grief in not knowing how someone died, in having not been present. Knowing doesn't necessarily fix anything and may leave you with new questions and new losses, but the urge to have the story finished is strong.

When the motorcyclist died in front of me—the tall man's voice rising, *"Is he dead? Is he dead? Oh, God,"* pacing back and forth by the tangle of broken bike, his words beginning to squeak as his throat closed until he walked to a tree, knelt, leaned his drooping head against the bark, and began to sob, loud and ragged—I wondered if his family would want details. I thought the tall man might want to talk about what had happened. By then I had found out that his father was in one of my exercise classes, and that he had attended the same high school as my daughter. I told myself that I would go to the funeral in case his father and friend wanted to know more of the story of his death. But in fact it was me that wanted to know the story of his life. I had seen only his face dead, inside a motorcycle helmet: glazed eyes, scruffy facial hair, a big nose. The photo with the obituary added big, uneven teeth, crow's-feet, a smile. I wanted to know who this man had been.

The church was crowded. I thought he might be one kind of

biker, but he turned out to be another. The church was filled with young people with pink and green hair and piercings and a lot of good ink. There were quite a few long-haired, bearded guys who cried into their leather sleeves, and my entire water aerobics class sharing a pew. It was a traditional Catholic funeral with lots of standing up and reciting and praying, and a sermon about eternal life. The program had a Mary Oliver poem: "I thought the earth / remembered me, she / took me back so tenderly." I didn't get the whole story, but I got enough.

In her memoir of dying (called *Dying: A Memoir*), Cory Taylor felt something lacking as she approached her own death. She was not religious, and realized that without a religious structure, there were few social frames for grief. "We have lost our common rituals and our common language for dying, and must either improvise, or fall back on traditions about which we feel deeply ambivalent. I am talking especially about people like me, who have no religious faith. For us it seems that dying exposes the limitations of secularism like nothing else." Atheism or agnosticism shouldn't mean no rituals; we hold rituals as a community and we create rituals out of our lives. Brushing your teeth is a ritual; chances are you do it exactly the same way every day. I believe in rituals and so I believe in funerals and wakes and memorials and doing these things on anniversaries and doing them with others. Ceremonies are one of the hinges of a community.

They can take any form you like. My friend Patrick arranged a potlatch for after his death. He didn't have much in the way of possessions, but everyone who knew him recognized the Hawaiian shirts, the sandals, the reading glasses. All his worldly goods were laid out on tables as though at a church bazaar. His friends wandered about, picking and choosing their favorites, making trades.

*   *   *

Sometimes grief isn't recognized; others don't understand why you grieve, or grieve with such passion. The loss seems relatively small: a divorced partner, a spouse with end-stage dementia, an early miscarriage. (Try explaining to your supervisor that your religious teacher has died and you need a few days off work.) There are no bereavement fares for a best friend or business partner. People may not even realize you are grieving: a secret affair may never be divulged, but the loss is real. This is sometimes called disenfranchised grief. Grief unrecognized or undervalued is real and disabling.

After unexpected or violent deaths, the survivors may feel what is commonly known as complicated grief: pain that remains sharp and unchanging for many months or years. I'm a little wary of this label, because grief has no strict timeline, no prescribed schedule in which one moves forward. But most people do move forward over several months or a few years, even if they think of the dead person every day. A new life without the person in it is slowly created.

My friends Thomas and Kevin moved across the country, from Oregon to Vermont, when Thomas was promoted. He called me early one morning, stunned: "Kevin's dead." Thomas had confronted him the evening before with his suspicions that Kevin was abusing drugs. Kevin carried a lot of demons, had anxiety and depression from a brutal childhood, and had abused both alcohol and prescription drugs in the past. Thomas didn't really want to believe he was doing it again, especially since he'd been diagnosed with heart disease and had a stent placed. But Kevin admitted it.

This is what Thomas remembers now, six years later: "I was just crestfallen. And as the afternoon wore on, he was popping more pills, and he was stumbling around." Thomas decided to get out of the house. He had dinner, went to a movie, and drove around town for several hours. "I came home," he remembers, "and the lights were on. The house looked normal, and I took the dog out and started closing house. I just assumed he was asleep upstairs. But when I went upstairs, he was not in bed, and I just panicked." He found Kevin in the basement laundry room with his face in a hamper full of clothes. "I remember thinking a mix of disbelief and 'This is it. It happened. This is how it happened.'" The dryer door was open and the light was on. "I reached over, half out of denial, half not knowing what you do. Do you touch him? Do you *not* touch him?" Thomas pulled him over and his body was already so stiff that he didn't lie flat. "He was dead, and had been dead for a while. He died doing *chores*! He was doing chores, he was self-medicating with Oxycontin, he was doing laundry."

He called the police. He didn't go back down to the basement and he never saw Kevin's body again, a choice he still regrets.

Thomas remembers that the police were kind. But they questioned him for a long time, taking turns. "'Where were you? Did anybody see you? Can anybody verify you were there? Do you have receipts?' You shift between extraordinary grief and pain the likes of which I didn't know you could feel, and complete denial the next moment, and task-oriented mode the next minute."

Kevin was found with two items in his pocket: a half-full bottle of Oxycontin and an AA sobriety chip. The medical examiner ruled the death accidental, a cardiac arrest related to the drug use. Kevin was thirty-nine years old.

The grief counselors John James and Russell Friedman developed a program they call Grief Recovery Method, based on James's experiences after his three-day-old baby died. Their work is based on the idea that unresolved grief happens because "the griever is often left with things they wish had happened *differently*, *better, or more*, and with unrealized *hopes, dreams, and expectations* for the future." This can be true in healthy relationships as well as dysfunctional ones, anticipated deaths as well as sudden ones. The relationship feels suspended, unfinished, with no way forward. Recovery means, to James and Friedman, letting go of "a different or better yesterday."

Thomas's loss was made worse by the fact that he was isolated. He took a promotion and moved. But he couldn't sustain himself by himself; he quit his job not long afterward and returned to Oregon.

He remembers three things said to him soon after the death that eventually became "game-changers," and they weren't the "soft, sweet, reassuring" comments. Kyogen, who was Thomas's religious teacher as well as mine, asked him if he was meditating. Thomas replied that it was too painful. "And he said, 'You must turn toward it.' I knew this! But he said it to me at my darkest hour, when I was most afraid, when I was petrified at seeing the reality of this. Another thing he said to me, later on, when I was talking about what a wonderful man Kevin was, he said, 'Yes, and when we remember Kevin, it's important that we remember *all* of Kevin.'"

James and Friedman recommend writing a detailed history of the relationship: highs, lows, successes, failures, resentments, joys. Finally, James and Friedman suggest writing the dead person a letter (never to be shown to anyone): a "*completion* letter rather than a *farewell* letter." The relationship as it was is over. Completed. The relationship, however complicated, was whole, had a beginning, middle, and end, had good times and bad. C. S. Lewis, in his short, devastating memoir about the loss of his wife, wrote, "Bereavement is not the truncation of married love but one of its regular phases—like the honeymoon."

The third thing Thomas remembers helping the most is something I said to him a few days after the death. "I would say to you on the phone, 'Why did I leave that night? He was not in good shape. Why did I stay gone for three and a half hours? Why didn't I turn around and come back? Did he do it on purpose? I should have known better. What did I not see—what, what, what?' And you said to me in a very firm voice, 'These things happen and you don't get to be different.' It had become a theme: it shouldn't have happened; why hadn't I known? That was your point. People miss things. This is just the quandary of life and it's as messy for you as for anybody else. Who are you to think that you are exempt from this? It was almost like being slapped through the phone. But it was the right medicine at the right time."

I don't remember this conversation; we spoke a lot on the phone in the first few weeks. I can imagine saying this because I believe it—that we want so desperately to revisit the moment when everything changed, and change it back, change it into something else, change ourselves, change the one who died. It's just that what we want isn't what happened. I can imagine saying this, because I know I've needed to hear it said.

He tells me now, that after three years, "I was just exhausted, carrying this around, and I thought I had to do something." He started therapy and one of the first things the counselor had him do was write to Kevin regularly.

*   *   *

After my mother died, I went through a gradual recovery. All James and Friedman are telling us is to consciously do what people have always done with death. Experience it. I talked to her, I looked at photos, I read letters, I talked to myself, I talked to (and I am sure that I bored) my friends. I told a lot of stories, silently and out loud, about my mother at different times of our life together, her past before I knew her, how she handled her illness, her career as a teacher.

Our relationship improved. We didn't argue anymore—which is to say, I didn't argue with her anymore. She listened to me and I told her secrets. As time went on— years, decades—my ideas about her and myself, about mothers and daughters, changed. My memories grew a bit rosy; I had fantasies about what my life would have been like if she'd lived longer. She'd have known her grandchildren, enjoyed her retirement. In my mind she outlives my father and we go to Reno and she gambles all day and we drink martinis by the pool in the summer evening. Happy fantasies. But I know they are fantasies; they are no longer regrets.

Kobayashi Issa was a famous Buddhist haiku poet in Japan's Edo period. After two of his children died in a short time—two of many losses he would suffer—Issa wrote this poem:

The world of dew
is a world of dew,
and yet, and yet

Dew, fleeting and fragile, is the nature of life. While we understand, somehow, that this is precisely what love is—that the china bowl is beautiful precisely because it will break, that we love each other because we do not live forever—we can barely imagine what that means.

A common phrase on nineteenth-century tombstones went: "It is a fearful thing to love what death can touch." A part of us holds back from love, always protecting itself, selfish, uncertain. After a death, there is no longer anything to fear. At last. At last, we lose that which we want most to keep. Then there is nothing more to lose. Then the human fears that drive us apart—our concern for the opinion of others, our pride, our shame—are revealed to be so very small. We see what really matters. And when we contemplate the one we have lost, our hearts are free of hesitation, holding nothing back. Grief is the opportunity to cherish another without reservation. Grief is the breath after the last one.

12

Joy

On the day I helped to sort Kyogen's bones, I came home tender
and raw. But I felt well. I felt remarkably strong and well. The
heavy, demanding *no*—the *No!* that had consumed me— dissolved
like cloud and smoke. I was riding a slow wave in a warm ocean.
I had held my teacher's bones in my hands, and I had heard him
laughing: his demented titter and his great guffaw and his happiness. That night, in the strange hypnagogic stillness before sleep,
I had a waking dream. I saw his life in a flickering rush: his face
both young and old, laughing, serious, silent, thoughtful; his slow,
nodding attention while I talked; his dead body; the decaying left-
overs; the coffin sliding into the furnace; the tray of bones. All this
flashed past me, disappearing as I watched. We are a loose collection glued briefly into a provisional thing called self, and all such
things are bound to dissolution. *How could this be otherwise?* I can
still hear him chuckling beside me. *What did you expect?* he asks.
And I laugh, because he's right. These bits of bone. How obvious
and whole.

When I first began to practice Buddhism, I was told a traditional story about a wanderer who was chased off a cliff by a tiger.
He caught a root and dangled there, listening to the tiger pace and

growl above him. When he looked down, there was a tiger below as well. Then he noticed a wild strawberry growing from a crevice nearby. What to do but pluck it? He ate with relish. In some versions of this story, the strawberry is just out of reach unless the wanderer lets go of the root.

I was startled to discover recently that Tolstoy tells this story, too. In his version, a person escapes from a wild animal by jumping into a well, only to discover that a dragon lives at the bottom. He hangs on to a root between beast and dragon and sees that a mouse is nibbling at the root. Then he sees a few drops of honey on a leaf and leans over to drink. Tolstoy recounts this fable in despair, but I remember being strangely consoled when I heard the story. I was in my early twenties and I was healthy, but I was plagued by anxiety. I could see that strawberry, but I couldn't reach it. It was some years more before I realized how close the berry is, and that all that was missing was my willingness to put out my hand.

We are nothing more than a collection of parts, and each part is a collection of smaller parts, and smaller still, the things we love and all we cherish only aggregations. We are put together from other things and will be taken apart and those things and what we become will in turn be taken apart and built anew. There is nothing known that escapes this fate. And knowing the answer does not stop the question from being asked. The blocks were built up; they will be taken apart the same way; we are nothing more. And yet we *are* something more; this is one of the mysteries, I know. I cannot point to the answer or name it, except in the limited and awkward ways I have already tried. There is something more, and it is the totality of this *nothing more*.

What do we call beautiful? New flowers in spring, autumn's

brilliant color, the cast of twilight across a mountainside. Beauty is most poignant at the moment it begins to fade. Twilight disappears as we watch. We love our endangered lives, these swift, fleeting lives, changing before our eyes. Life as it is. Luminous, everyday, extraordinary life. Do we always know that with every birth comes a death? That the most tender and complete meeting has to end? We see the beauty of all that will break and leave us—a brief touch, a breath, a glance, a sip of water, the glowing leaves falling from the trees, the ones we love, and our own life. Strawberry. A single strawberry, plucked from the earth, damp with dew and red as a heart.

In the spring, a few months after Carol died, I was thinking of her. I thought of her every day that season. Spring in Oregon can be so lovely, you catch your breath between one step and the next. I had spent a few days in the rolling hills not far away from where she'd lived, and been struck by how insistently the world was calling out. So many voices. I found a little lime-green frog in the shower, and watched a bald eagle circle over the meadow for a long time. I saw a hatchling of ants and weeded the lettuce, all the time listening to the voices of the world. Flowers and insects, grass and birds and people calling out, *Here I am.*

When I got home, I found a message from David. He'd written to say that a bird had made a nest on Carol's grave and laid four small white eggs. The nest was beside where her pillow would have been. Carol's pillow had been made into a nest. I thought, *She would love it,* and then I thought, *Maybe she does.* Maybe she is laughing at us all right now, saying, *Here I am.* She is gone away and isn't coming back, but instead: Ant. Frog. Eagle. Egg.

I've never felt better.

Appendix 1:

Preparing a Death Plan

W e make a death plan because we can—for our own peace of mind, and as an act of compassion for the people nearest to us who will be left, quite literally, holding things.

Where and how do you want to die? Plan for your ideal. It could happen! You may prefer your own bedroom or a small cabin in the woods. Think about all the details. Do you like wind chimes? Do you like *Judge Judy*? Do you want to watch *Duck Soup*? Make a death-bed playlist (and don't forget comedy). Do you want any religious services? Should religion be banned? Do you want to be touched, and by whom? How much solitude do you want? Who is not to be admitted?

And once you've made a lot of these decisions, choose one or two people to be the gatekeepers. Who is willing to turn Aunt Agatha away, play the Ramones at high volume, and dress you in that cunning miniskirt at the last moment?

Everyone needs a will, no matter how much they own. The will must be signed and witnessed and dated. Your will describes in detail the way your money is to be distributed and any specific bequests and donations. It should name an executor you trust to dispose of your body and your possessions as you ask. Does your will explain what should happen to your personal possessions? To whom do you want to leave photographs, works of art, letters, jewelry, and diaries? Is there anything you want destroyed? What happens to your prize roses, your lingerie, and the old family photos? Many authors have declared that unfinished manuscripts, journals, and notes should be destroyed. Terry Pratchett declared that the hard drive holding his unfinished books was to be smashed by a steamroller, and so it was done.

You might write letters to your family members and friends and put them in the same folder. They don't need to be long or fancy letters; just say goodbye and maybe add a little advice or encouragement. Write new letters every year. You may want to compose your obituary.

Don't forget pets. Don't forget outstanding bills, automatic payments, online accounts and passwords, and all the people who need to know you died. Remember electronic dating profiles, Second Life avatars, the bridge club, the gym, and the dentist. Who can get access to your calendar? If you are someone else's health care representative, include that information in your death plan, because they need to find someone else now. Who has access to your checking accounts, brokerage accounts, and safe deposit box? (Is your will *in* your safe deposit box? Bad place for it.)

If you are a professional who keeps confidential records—a teacher, therapist, lawyer, accountant, minister—do you have a written plan for how to handle those records? Do you have a list of clients to contact and a partner to take over your appointments? Who pays the bills and does the books for the business? Think about office keys, passwords, file cabinets, and storage units.

The following document is intended to help you consider the details that may be important to you in your final days. Give copies to your physician, executor, family members, health care representatives, lawyer, and religious teacher.

MY DEATH PLAN

Contact Information

Legal name: _____

Phone number: _____

Today's date: _____

Emergency Contacts

Name: _____

Phone number: _____

Email: _____

Relationship: _____

Street address: _____

Name: _____

Phone number: _____

Email: _____

Relationship: _____

Street address: _____

Primary Care Provider

Name: _____

Phone number: _____

Organization: _____

Specialist Doctor

Name: _____

Phone number: _____

Organization: _____

Documents

I have an advance directive: YES   NO
Location: _____

I have a POLST (physician's order for life-sustaining treatment) form: YES   NO
Location: _____

I have a do-not-resuscitate (DNR) order that is separate from the POLST order: YES   NO
Location: _____

I have a health care power of attorney: YES   NO
Location: _____

I have a financial power of attorney: YES   NO
Location: _____

I have a will: YES   NO
Location: _____

I would like to be an organ donor: YES   NO
Any restrictions (eyes only, all organs, etc.)? _____
_____

I would like to be a tissue donor (middle-ear bones, heart valves, corneas, bones, etc.):   YES   NO

<u>End-of-Life Wishes</u>

I would like to die in the following place: _____

_____

As I am dying, I would like visits from: _____

_____

I would like visits dedicated to formal religious practice from (please describe): _____

_____

_____

With respect, I do not want to see: _____

_____

When I am close to dying, I would like the following forms of support and comfort (people, readings, rituals, music, food, scents, sights, etc.): _____

_____

_____

If pain can only be controlled with a dose that sedates me to the point of being unable to engage in conversation:

I do want my pain completely controlled even if I am sedated: YES   NO

I would prefer to be awake and manage a moderate level of pain: YES   NO

When death is imminent, I would like the following rituals or services: _____

_____

_____

_____

At the moment of death, I would like the following rituals or services: _____

_____

_____

After death, I would like the following rituals or services: _____

_____

_____

_____

Disposal of My Body

After my death, my preference for handling of my body: _____

_____

_____

_____

My preferred funeral home or crematorium: _____

_____

My preferred cemetery or burial place: _____

_____

I have money set aside for disposal of my body: YES   NO
Location: _____

Special Circumstances

Do you have any confidential records or other documents in your care (e.g., therapist records, legal records, teacher-student correspondence) that should be protected or destroyed? If so, please describe the general nature of the materials, where they are located, and what should be done with them. _____

_____

_____

_____

If you have clients, who can contact them and arrange for new appointments? _____

_____

_____

Do you have any religious objects or vestments that should be handled in a particular way or given to a specific person? _____

_____

_____

_____

I am the executor or personal representative for: _____

_____

SIGNED: _____

NAME: _____

DATE: _____

WITNESS: _____

DATE: _____

WITNESS: _____

DATE: _____

Copies of this plan are on file with: _____

_____

Appendix 2:

Advance Directives

A third of Americans over sixty-five will spend time in an ICU in the three months before they die, facing surgery or other aggressive treatments intended to keep them living as long as possible. I doubt if they all really want to do that. The same people who say they have thought a great deal about their wishes at the end of life have never discussed those wishes with their doctor or family, or even written them down.

An *advance directive* (sometimes called a *living will*) is a form in which you explain what you want done to save or prolong your life if you are unable to make decisions for yourself. The directive includes questions about ventilators, tube feeding, antibiotics, and other life-supporting treatments. Many people assume that advance directives have legal weight. They do not. The directive is intended to *advise* your treating doctors and representative in making appropriate choices. It also protects health care professionals and representatives from charges of neglect or mistreatment if they follow your wishes.

One of the problems with advance directives is that many people have little experience with death and don't understand the repercussions of treatments that may be called for in a life-threatening emergency or terminal illness. You may have an un-realistic idea of your own willingness to tolerate illness, loss of function, or aggressive medical care. A person who is familiar with aggressive medical treatment can err on the other side. My own inclination is to say, *No ventilator, ever,* but there are times when a short-term ventilator makes sense, such as after trauma to the chest. The directive should be nuanced.

The advance directive helps you to consider the many pos-sibilities that may arise. There are different versions of the direc-tive from state to state, with more or less granularity. The one I've filled out, for Oregon, starts with a section called *Close to Death*:

If I am close to death and life support would only postpone the moment of my death:

A. INITIAL ONE:

_____ I want to receive tube feeding.

_____ I want tube feeding only as my physician recommends.

_____ I DO NOT WANT tube feeding. (Capital letters included.)

B. INITIAL ONE:

_____ I want any other life support that may apply.

_____ I want life support only as my physician recommends.

_____ I want NO life support.

This is followed by sections titled Permanently Unconscious, Advanced Progressive Illness, and Extraordinary Suffering, with the same options for each. There is a further section for General Instructions that allows you to reiterate your wishes and gives you room to be as detailed as you can.

An advance directive from the United Kingdom goes into significantly more detail about forms of pain and suffering, incapacity, immobility, physical helplessness, burdens to family and loved ones, and specific medical interventions, including artificial nutrition and hydration, bladder catheterization, enemas, being hand-fed, and respiratory support. I would prefer to use this one, and intend to add this kind of detail to my state's directive. As an example, the UK directive includes these options:

My reaction to profound dementia to the point where I can no longer recognise my loved ones and interact with them in a coherent fashion:

_____ intolerable; I prefer death
_____ a very negative factor, to be weighed with other factors in determining intolerable indignity
_____ tolerable

Many people will find such questions easy to answer, but it's easy to get hung up, argue with the wording, and ask what-if questions. Think about how you define *quality of life*, and consider illness, pain, disability and dependence, cognitive decline, and specific symptoms like having trouble breathing. Consider addressing specific treatments like dialysis, ventilators, antibiotics, sedation, and pain control. Become familiar with the possibilities.

After you fill out the form, there is space to add a short statement about why you answered as you did. This is a really important part of the form. Define your personal values around life and death so that your representative and doctors can understand your intent. Explain your reasons in detail. Life-threatening situations usually require sets of related decisions, not a single choice. Knowing your reasons will help guide the people who must make decisions under the pressure of time and strong emotion.

The advance directive allows you to appoint a health care representative who is empowered to make decisions for you if you cannot. In spite of all the complicated chores my friend Thomas had to handle after Kevin died, he didn't have to fight for the right to do so. They weren't married but they had done all the paperwork: wills, advance directives, health care representative, and powers of attorney.

Be sure you choose a representative who understands and accepts your wishes, is truly willing to carry your wishes forward, *and* can be assertive in the face of emergent decisions and pressure from medical providers who might disagree with your hopes. Be sure that your health care representative is comfortable making hard choices and not easily cowed. It really can't be emphasized enough that your representative needs to be willing to *be your representative*, to speak for you when you can't speak for yourself. If your answer is no, the representative must be willing to say no. If a doctor balks at the representative's wishes, the representative can ask the doctor to step aside. If a hospital balks at the representative's requests—which may happen in a religious institution—the representative can request a transfer to another hospital or simply a discharge. A medical ethicist has done research into why doctors sometimes don't follow advance directives, and has found two main reasons. The first is that the document is too vague or asks for the impossible. The second reason, he adds, "is that the doctor is a jerk and is practicing unethical medicine." If the representative feels blocked in fulfilling the advance directives, he or she can demand to speak to the quality assurance department or ask for an ethics consult. The last resort is a judge.

Don't choose a representative who works on your health care team or anyone employed by the institution or agency providing treatment. (They should know better, anyway.) Don't choose a person who works for an agency helping to pay for your care. Be very wary about choosing a member of your immediate family. A friend who knows your values and can handle a crisis is ideal. John Abraham, an Episcopal priest who has done death education for decades, suggests you find a person who "is able to refuse useless medical efforts, exhibit moxie and equanimity when under stress, and not capitulate when confronted" by recalcitrant staff. The representative, he adds, should be someone who "can be a 'son-of-a-bitch.'"

Have a frank and detailed conversation with your primary doctor now, if you can. You may have to block the door of the exam room to do this. Many doctors do not allow for the kind of time such a conversation requires, and they are poorly compensated when they do. If you can't pin your doctor down on his beliefs about end-of-life care, consider changing doctors. If he or she won't make time to talk to you now, while you're still walking around and eating your oatmeal, what's going to happen when you're fading out and everyone's shouting? You deserve to talk about it first.

If you are ill or frail, have another detailed conversation about the risks, benefits, and possible outcomes of your treatment. What can be anticipated? What cannot? You may be looking at radiation, chemotherapy, blood transfusions, tube feeding, and breathing support, as well as the possibility of resuscitation. All are possible treatments for a person with a serious illness, and all have risks as well as benefits. What are the side effects? What are the rare and probably-will-never-happen events that could lead to someone having to make a crucial decision in a hurry?

Talk to your partner, your children, and your parents. If a particular member of your family strongly disagrees with your choice, don't include them in the conversation. If you are concerned about their influence, name that person on your form as someone who is not allowed to make decisions for you and perhaps should not be involved in any meetings with your doctor. This isn't the time to worry about hurting Aunt Josie's feelings.

The directive does you no good if it is hidden in a drawer or locked in a safe deposit box, is many years out of date, or names a representative who is either no longer close to you, unaware that he or she is your representative, or uncomfortable with your wishes. After you fill out an advance directive, give a copy to your primary care physician, to the health care representatives you've named, and to a few close family and friends. Then talk about it. It's a good idea to sign and date the directive every few years, and again if you become ill, so that decision makers are aware that these are recent wishes and not the fantasy of long ago.

A second form that may be available to you is called the *POLST, physician's order for life-sustaining treatment*. Oregon was the first state to offer POLST, and it is now widely available. This is a legal doctor's order that defines how much and what kind of life support you want to receive if you can't make a decision for yourself. Its use is restricted to people in poor health. This is the form that will have the most immediate influence on critical medical decisions about aggressive life support such as CPR and ventilators. Often a POLST—usually bright pink and hard to miss—will be posted on the refrigerator in a person's home, and paramedics know to look for it. The POLST should travel with the person when they go to the hospital. You can even carry a small version in a necklace or bracelet. The POLST is now electronic in Oregon as well: http://polst.org

You might also want to designate a person to act as your *durable power of attorney for health care*. This is a legal representative who can make any and all treatment decisions for you if you cannot, whether or not you have an advance directive. The National Hospice and Palliative Care Organization provides links to the advance directive form recognized in each state: http://www.caringinfo .org/i4a/pages/index.cfm?pageid=3289.

Appendix 3:

Organ and Tissue Donation

Donating any part of the body is best planned well in advance. In the United States, when a person dies in a hospital, the staff is required to ask about organ donation, but not everyone is a candidate. Each case will be considered individually, so don't hesitate to ask. There is no age limit, and people can be donors even if they have a serious illness. If you are with a person who is a tissue, organ, or whole-body donor, be prepared to contact the donor help line as soon as possible after death.

Eyes can be donated by almost everybody. Donor eyes are used to cure corneal blindness as well as in research. They are harvested within six hours of death. The procedure is quick, discreet, and not disfiguring.

Almost everyone can be a tissue donor, and tissues can be recovered several hours after death. Tissues are used in several ways: heart valves and middle-ear bones are transplanted, tendons are used in knee surgeries, and skin is used for burns. Ground-up bone can be used to make dental implants or replace lost bone. Be aware that donated tissue may also be used in for-profit procedures like cosmetic surgery, and when you decide to be a donor, you may not know how it will be used.

Tissue donation can be done in two ways. You can do a whole-body donation in which organs and cells are taken and distributed to research laboratories and universities. In this case the body will be cremated within a few weeks and the ashes returned to the family. You can also have specific tissues removed and the body returned within a day for burial or cremation.

A person may become an organ donor when he or she enters an irreversible condition they cannot survive, such as a massive cardiac arrest that destroys the heart's ability to function. Such a person is called a "non-heart-beating donor." After the proxy decides to stop aggressive support and allow natural death to occur, the person is taken to an operating room. The ventilator and drugs are stopped, the person is declared dead, and organs are removed immediately.

Brain death can be caused by any permanent large brain injury, such as a massive stroke or trauma. Brain death (now often called total brain failure) is an objective, quantifiable state. A coma alone is not brain death: people often recover from a coma. In brain death, there is no possibility of recovery. A persistent vegetative state is not brain death. A person in a vegetative state has a functioning brain stem but no conscious activity in the brain itself. They have reflexive, uncontrolled physical movements and sleep and wake cycles, and may make sounds, but are not conscious in any way.

The first step in diagnosis is determining the cause and ruling out conditions that can mimic brain death, like poisoning or hypothermia. Then the person is stabilized as much as possible: electrolyte imbalances are corrected, body temperature and blood volume are corrected, and blood pressure is brought to normal, usually with drugs. The set of tests done to determine the diagnosis may vary from one hospital to another, but a generally accepted set of criteria is used. The diagnosis is made over hours or days by a team of specially trained physicians who have no personal interest in the result. (Physicians who might be involved in organ transplantation do not participate in the diagnosis.)

A lot of people assume that brain death is proven with a flat electroencephalogram (EEG) measurement (poetically known as electrocerebral silence). It's an important part of the exam but not sufficient, as a few other conditions can cause a flat EEG, like hypothermia. Tests are done for any response to stimulation and reflexes moderated by the brain, such as stroking the cornea of the eye. A body without a functioning brain may still move in primitive ways, due to reactions in the spinal cord and peripheral nerves. The face, fingers, toes, and arms may contract and the entire trunk may shiver and twist. A particular contraction of the neck muscles can cause a body to almost sit up or turn the head to one side; this is known as the "Lazarus sign."

All these tests may be repeated more than once. Finally, an apnea test is performed. While the body—which may yet be a person; that's what's being tested—is still getting oxygen, the ventilator is disconnected. If the body makes no effort to breathe for about ten minutes, that's an important proof.

People with brain death continue to have a heartbeat, because the heart has its own pacemaker and often will continue to beat as long as there is oxygen, though the person will require advanced support such as ventilators and drugs to maintain blood pressure. The brain manages the critical functions of the body. Even with a beating heart, almost everyone diagnosed with brain death has what is known as "somatic death" within a week: the organs and systems simply collapse, unable to function. If organs are going to be donated, it is usually done soon after the diagnosis is reached.

I have hesitated throughout this discussion between the words *person* and *body*. Brain death is death. A person on a ventilator with a beating heart and brain death has died. The phrase sometimes used is *beating-heart cadaver*. A neurologist says that he tries to avoid the term *life support* in a brain-dead person, because it confuses the issue. He prefers *organ support*.

That is the textbook explanation. This is how it sometimes goes: My friend Stephanie was a primary care physician in a small town. The last time I saw her, she talked passionately about the number of people with diabetes and poor nutrition, and her ideas for how to fix everything. Stephanie was a fixer of problems, idealistic about the possibility of doing so, and impatient to get on with it.

The whole town was covered in a big snowstorm, and she decided to go sledding with her fiancé and friends. She slid down a long hill into an intersection and was hit by a truck. Her injuries were massive, and the phrase *no hope of recovery* was used almost immediately. The Life Flight helicopter was able to get her to the nearest trauma center. Her parents were in another state, enjoying a sunny vacation. They couldn't get back because of the storms; they waited in airports and hotels for days while flight after flight was canceled.

This is how it usually goes: not organs but a person. A life. And an excruciating choice. Stephanie's parents were finally able to make it to the hospital, and a day later announced that she had died and been an organ donor—"her last gift," in her father's words.

Three months earlier, my friend Jaime had received a new liver, perhaps from someone a lot like Stephanie.

Appendix 4:

Assisted Death

Assisted death is the act of giving a dying person the means by which that person can kill himself. There are many terms for assisted death: *assistance in dying, aid in dying, physician-assisted death, death with dignity*. All of these are more accurate terms than *assisted suicide*. I choose the term *assisted death*; the act is emphatically a choice, yet nothing like suicide as we generally understand it.

The word *euthanasia* means "good death." Euthanasia is the act of killing a person or animal out of mercy, because the person is hopelessly suffering or terminally ill. Euthanasia is legal in several countries, but in most cases it is more exactly physician-assisted death. The choice is consciously made by the dying person rather than by a doctor or proxy acting independently.

I live in Oregon, the first state—and one of the first governments in the world—to make assisted death legal. Assisted death is now legal in the states of Washington, Montana, Colorado, New Mexico, Vermont, and California, as well as several European countries, Canada, and Australia. By the time this is published, I suspect the list will have grown. The Netherlands, Belgium, and Luxembourg allow a form of euthanasia or physician-assisted death for people who are not terminally ill but experience "un-bearable suffering." In the United States and Switzerland, the situation is the opposite: a person must be terminally ill but need not express unbearable suffering.

In Oregon, you must be expected to die within six months, be at least eighteen years of age, and be making the decision for yourself. The most common two reasons for choosing assisted death in Oregon are cancer and amyotrophic lateral sclerosis (ALS). A person must make two verbal requests at least fifteen days apart, and also a written request signed by two witnesses. At that point, the person is given counseling on palliative care and hospice. The law requires that the person can take the medication independently, even if other people are in the room. The drug used is usually Seconal, or secobarbital sodium.

Canada recently passed a medical-assistance-in-dying law after years of heated discussion. A person must be over eighteen years of age, mentally competent, have a "grievous and irremediable medical condition," and be able to give informed consent. The grievous condition does not have to be terminal, but it has to be advanced and irreversible, and the person must be at such a point that "natural death has become reasonably foreseeable." A written request signed by two witnesses is submitted and followed by a "10-day reflection period." The law also requires people to be capable of consenting in the moment of death: they must sign a form just before the procedure stating they have had a chance to change their mind and want to continue. In Canada, the doctor administers the medication, either by mouth or intravenously. (Almost everyone chooses the injection.) The drugs are a combination of midazolam, an antianxiety drug that makes people sleepy, a little lidocaine to numb the vein, followed by propofol, an anesthetic that puts people into a coma. Finally, the doctor administers ro-curonium, which causes paralysis. In virtually all cases, the heart stops within a few minutes.

For any action, we can ask: What is the intent? In the recent past—and in certain places and conditions today—assistance in death may be a response to a lack of necessary care. But in the West, we are more likely to suffer from an excess of complex care. Intention is the best way to judge the morality of a choice in such ambiguous conditions. Being ready to die because of illness or disability is not the same as the desire to die. Turning toward assisted death is a way of accepting reality.

Autonomy is an important value for almost everyone, and lack of autonomy is one of the most common reasons for making this choice. I find it ironic that people will support a person's auton-omy throughout an illness and deny them the right to choose how the illness ends. If we believe that people must take responsibility for their own lives, moment by moment and day by day, we must allow people the room to make choices even if we think they are making a mistake. Each of us will face death eventually. Can any of us be so certain about its outcome that we can tell another how to behave at such a momentous time?

The most important aspect of the issue is whether we can ac-cept the real conditions before us. Can we face the very difficult choices life may bring? Can we allow others to face those difficult choices in their own way? A young friend of mine spent two years caring for her husband after his diagnosis of ALS. He had been a vigorous athlete, a rock climber. By the time he was in his mid-thirties, he was confined to a wheelchair and required almost total nursing care. He arranged for assisted death, but then—like many people—held on to the drugs for a time. One day he told his wife that he didn't think he would be able to swallow much longer. "Today's the day," he said. And it was. Assisted death can allow a person an opportunity that will slip away if he waits: the opportunity to be awake to the choice, to slide into death consciously.

Assisted death is deeply disliked by many medical and nursing professionals. Helping someone to die is simply immoral to some doctors. Other professionals believe that a doctor has no business deciding if a person's life has meaning and therefore they should have nothing to do with ending it. Some believe that palliative care can ease all the concerns that drive people to this choice. A few believe that anyone making the request to die should be assessed for mental illness. People who work in hospice and palliative care fall on both sides of the issue. Few are without an opinion. (One of the unintended consequences of such laws is that pharmaceutical companies are taking advantage; the price of the needed dose of Seconal approaches $4,000 now, and experts are working on new drug combinations that can be made by compounding pharmacies.)

In the Netherlands, between 2 and 3 percent of deaths are the result of physician assistance. Only a third of the people requesting euthanasia received it, either because they weren't found eligible or because they changed their mind. In a Dutch study, people with qualifying diseases were as likely *not* to request assistance in dying as to request it. The researchers believed that one of the main drivers for requesting euthanasia was to exert control over death in the only way possible.

Since the law passed in Canada, almost a thousand people have died this way (less than 1 percent of deaths). As in Oregon, most made the choice because of cancer or neurodegenerative diseases. The Canadian law is being challenged on several fronts. It requires doctors who don't want to participate to refer patients to doctors who will, which is seen by some people as an infringement on physicians' religious freedom. Patients are challenging the law because it prevents people with chronic disability whose death is not "reasonably foreseeable" from using it. The requirement that a person give consent at the last moment eliminates many people with dementia; some people who did qualify were eventually disqualified because they became too confused.

A discussion of assisted death is not theoretical; each of us may face such a choice, for ourselves or with someone we love. If you are uncomfortable with supporting assisted death for terminally ill people, there are many things you can do. Here, too, your volition is important: Is your intent to control another person, or to ease that person's suffering? You can volunteer as a companion to a dying person, or help a hospice or palliative care organization provide support. You can also make your own wishes for death and dying clear, an important way to reduce suffering for your family in the future.

The fear has been expressed, in Oregon and in every place such a law has been passed, that the law would be used to prey on vulnerable, poorly educated, or disabled people. Since the law passed in Oregon in 1997, a total of 1,749 people have made use of it; 1,127 people died this way. The average age was seventy-one. Patients were divided almost evenly between men and women, were overwhelmingly white, and almost all were high school or college graduates. Almost everyone died at home, and almost all were receiving hospice care. Most of the people who chose not to take the medication died from their disease or other causes. Many of the latter group said they were consoled by the fact that they had a choice, and were content to know they could end their life at the time of their choosing.

The information in *Advice for the Dying* is based on the US health care system and legislation. There are some differences in the United Kingdom, including in relation to the direct cost to patients of hospital care and palliative care, advance care planning, assisted dying and organ donation. There are also differences in legislation in relation to cannabis use and dealing with bodies. Brand names of some medications are different as well, as are prescription guidelines.

The following are resources for readers in the United Kingdom.

Bereavement Groups:

Bereavement Advice Centre: bereavementadvice.org
Bereavement Register (the names and addresses of the person who has died are removed from mailing lists, stopping most advertising mail within six weeks): thebereavementregister.org.uk
Bereavement Trust: bereavement-trust.org.uk
Cruse Bereavement Care: www.crusebereavementcare.org.uk and Hope Again (a sub-section of Cruse that provides support for children or teenagers dealing with loss): http://hopeagain.org.uk/
Dying Matters: https://www.dyingmatters.org/
Macmillan Cancer Support: https://www.macmillan.org.uk/
Maggie's Centres: https://www.maggiescentres.org/
Mencap (Support for people with learning disabilities and their families, including bereavement support): https://www.mencap.org.uk/
NHS Choices: https://www.nhs.uk/Livewell/bereavement/Pages/bereavement.aspx

Samaritans: www.samaritans.org.uk
Support After Suicide: https://supportaftersuicide.org.uk/
Support Line (Confidential and free emotional support for
    children, young adults and adults): http://supportline.org.uk/
Survivors of Bereavement by Suicide: https://uksobs.org/
The Compassionate Friends: https://www.tcf.org.uk/
The Loss Foundation: https://www.thelossfoundation.org/
WAY (Widowed and Young) Foundation: https://www.
    widowedandyoung.org.uk/

Child Bereavement Groups:

Barnardos Child Bereavement Service: http://www.barnardos.
    org.uk/childbereavementservice
Child Bereavement UK: https://childbereavementuk.org/
Grief Encounter: https://www.griefencounter.org.uk/
Lullaby Trust: https://www.lullabytrust.org.uk/
SANDS: https://www.sands.org.uk/
Saying Goodbye: https://www.sayinggoodbye.org/
Winston's Wish: http://www.winstonswish.org/

Funeral Arrangements:

Child Funeral Society: http://www.childfuneralcharity.org.uk/
Muslim Council of Britain: http://www.mcb.org.uk/
National Association of Funeral Directors: http://nafd.org.uk/
Natural Death Centre: http://www.naturaldeath.org.uk/
United Synagogue Burial Society: https://www.theus.org.uk/burial

Planning Ahead:

Final Choices: https://www.finalchoices.co.uk/
NHS end of life resources: https://www.nhs.uk/Planners/end-of-
    life-care/Pages/what-is-end-of-life-care.aspx
NHS organ donation website: https://www.organdonation.nhs.uk/

Acknowledgments

I am the student of the many people—friends, family, strangers, and clients—who have allowed me to enter into the extraordinary world of the dying and the dead. Each one has had a unique lesson to teach me, lessons I've learned imperfectly and incompletely. But I intend to keep studying.

My agent, Kim Witherspoon, has been a good friend as well as a blunt adviser for many years. I appreciate my editor, Lauren Spiegel, and all the team at Touchstone for steady support and careful reading.

I want to thank Jennifer Stoots for both efficient help with research and solid cheerleading when I needed it the most, Angie Jabine for careful reading, Jeanna Annen Moyer for helping me think through the death plan, and Rachel Wolf for her tremendous patience and humor. Much gratitude to N. Kathryn Moreland, MD, for careful reading and gentle corrections.

Portions of this book appeared in a different form in *Conjunctions, Tricycle,* and *Buddhadharma* magazines.

A shout-out to Mark Vanhoenacker, whose lovely book, *Skyfaring,* cured me of that last bit of fear of flying. I wish I could visit you in the cockpit.

Dennis Potter's remarkable BBC interview has been excerpted, with slight variations, in many works. The quote used here is from the transcript of the interview as published in *Seeing the Blossom* by Dennis Potter (Faber and Faber, 1994).

My dear friends: You know who you are. I hope you are there with me when the time comes.

About the Author

Sallie Tisdale is the author of several books, including *Violation*, *Talk Dirty to Me*, *Stepping Westward*, and *Women of the Way*. She has received a Pushcart Prize, an NEA Fellowship, and the James D. Phelan Literary Award and was selected for the Schoenfeldt Distinguished Visiting Writer Series. Her work has appeared in *Harper's*, *The New Yorker*, *The Threepenny Review*, *The Antioch Review*, *Conjunctions*, and *Tricycle*.